PHOTOGRAPH

PLAN

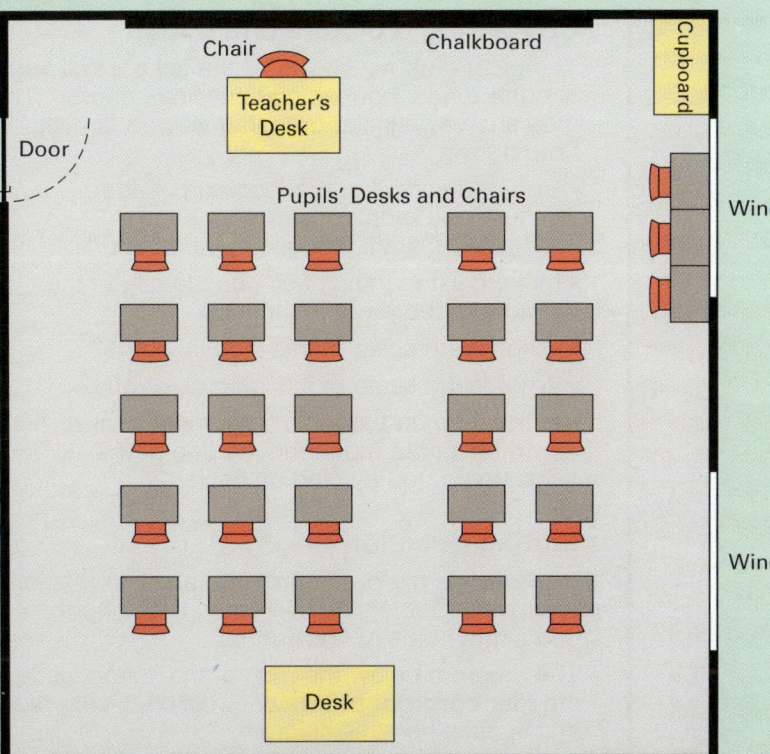

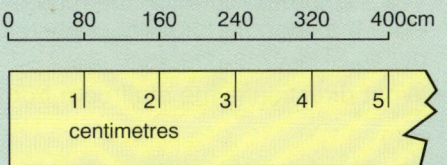

One centimetre on the plan is the same as 80 centimetres in the classroom

What is in the photograph?

The children in the photograph are learning atlas skills. They are finding out how many kilometres it is from one place to another using an atlas map. The teacher is helping one of the girls. Look carefully at the picture.

- Where is the chalkboard?
- List all the other things you can see.
- Do you have all these things in your own classroom?
- In which ways is your own classroom different?

What is in the plan?

The **plan** is a carefully prepared drawing. This plan shows what the classroom looks like if you look down on it directly from above. Try to match all the things in the plan with the things you can see in the photograph. How many can you match?

- How many pupil's desks are there in the plan?
- How many windows does the classroom have?
- What is represented by the black line around the plan?

Every plan has a scale

The photograph shows the classroom in a small rectangle. It is much smaller than the room itself. The plan is also drawn smaller than the actual size of the classroom. This is called drawing to **scale**. On the plan on this page, each centimetre on the page represents 80 centimetres in the classroom itself. This is known as a **line scale** and is shown by the special line above the yellow ruler.

- Use the line scale to work out how long the chalkboard is.
- Find out the length and breadth of the classroom using the line scale.

Every plan or map has its own scale.

- Find the landscape map of your own country in this atlas. How many kilometres are shown by one centimetre?

A plan is a large scale map

A plan is the word for a **map** drawn of a building or a lot of land. It is a very **large scale** map. One centimetre of this plan of the classroom shows just 80 centimetres of the real classroom. This ratio is 1:80. If the number on the right of the ratio is small, it is called a large scale map. If the number on the right of the ratio is a big number (such as 1:3,500,000 for the landscape map of Guyana on page 37), it is called a **small scale** map.

© Bartholomew Ltd.

2 A Map of the School

PICTURE

MAP

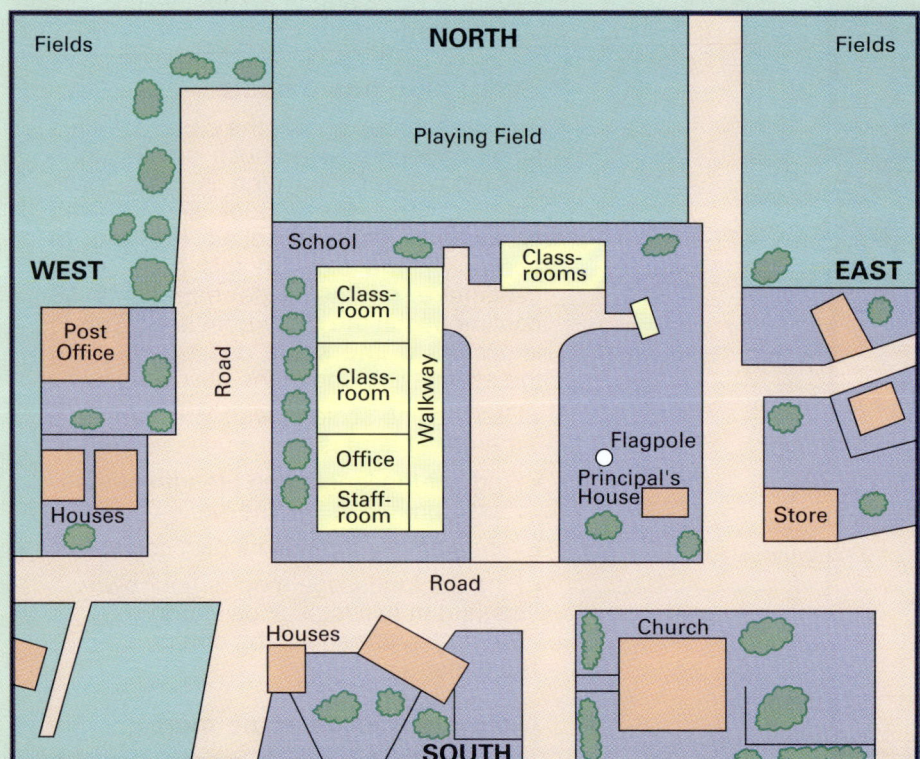

One centimetre on the map is the same as 12 metres on the ground

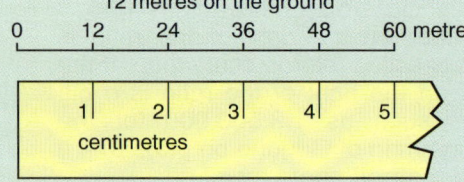

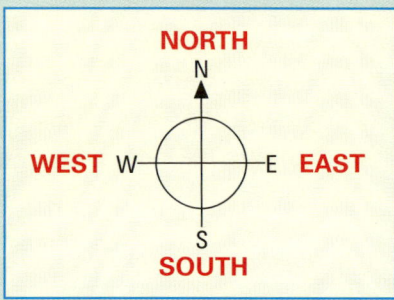

Comparing a picture and a map

The picture above shows all the school buildings and the roads, houses and buildings nearby. The map shows a similar area, but viewed directly from above.

- Can you find all of the following in both picture and map: a classroom block, the playing field, a flagpole, the post office?
- Make a list of things you can identify in the picture that are not in the map.
- What is the scale of this map in words?
- What is the scale of this map as a ratio?
- Is the map on the left a **larger scale** or a **smaller scale** map than the one of the classroom you studied on page 1?

Stating direction

Direction is the position of one place in relation to another. It is stated in relation to the north and south poles of the Earth.

The diagram below the map of the school shows the four **cardinal points** of direction. Every map in this atlas has this diagram.

- Find the diagram of cardinal points of direction on the map of the Caribbean on pages 8 and 9.

Use the map of the school on the left to work out the relative positions of the following:

- What is the direction on the map of the school from the flagpole to the goal posts on the playing field?
- What direction is the staffroom from the store?

A Smaller Scale Map   3

PHOTOGRAPH

MAP

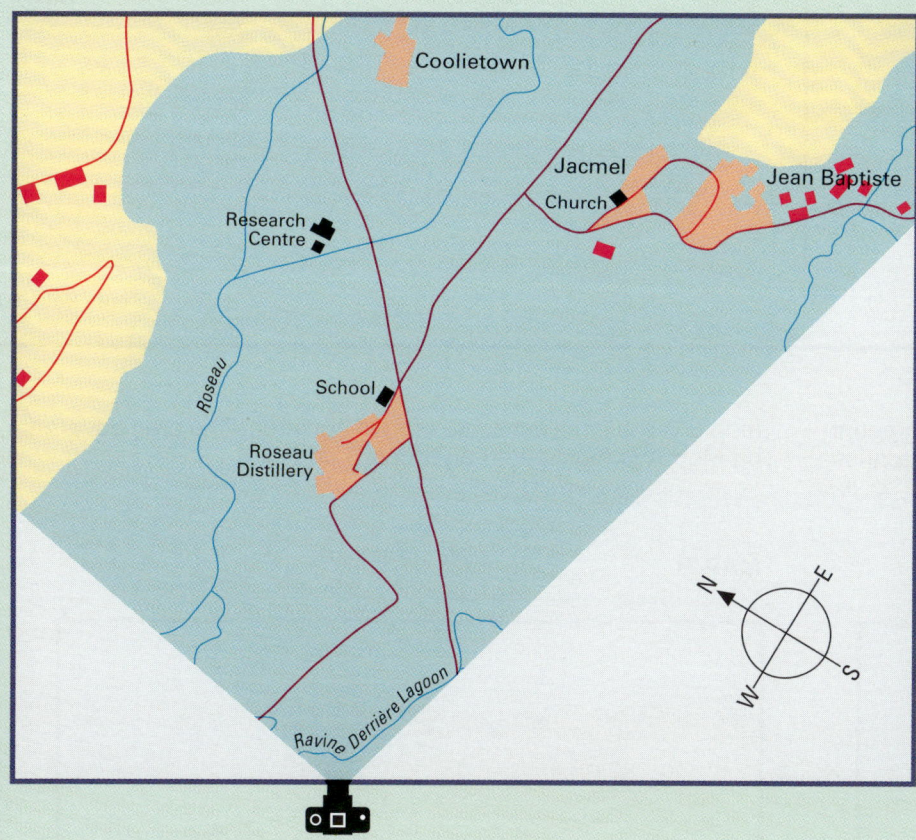

One centimetre on the map is the same as 200 metres on the ground

0 200 400 600 800 1000 metres

1 2 3 4 5 centimetres

- Town or village
- High land
- Low land
- Road
- Small farm
- Important building
- River

The area around a school

The map shows the area around a school. Part of this area can also be seen in the photograph. This map is drawn on a much smaller scale than the map on page 2, so it is more difficult to find the school, and no detail is shown. This time the school is shown as a black square. As scale gets smaller, detail gets less and less.

- Find the school on the map.
- How far is the school from the church?

Most maps have the direction north to the top of the map. This one does not: north is in the direction of the top left hand corner of the map. This is because the map was drawn to match the photograph.

- Can you work out the direction of the church at Jacmel from Coolietown?

Lines, symbols and colours

A **key** is found on every map to explain what things mean. The key may have lines, symbols and colours. Each kind of **line** will have a special meaning. So will each **symbol** and each **colour** used to tint part of the map. On this map, a road is shown as a red line although roads are not red in the photograph, nor in real life.

- What kind of symbol is used to show important buildings on this map?
- What kind of line is used to show rivers?
- What does green mean on this map?

A key is special to each individual map. You must check the key on each map that you use. Green, for example, will mean different things on different maps.

- What does green mean on the maps on pages 30 and 31?

© Bartholomew Ltd.

4 Latitude and Longitude

Lines of latitude

Lines of **latitude** circle the Earth in an east to west direction. They are drawn on maps but of course they do not exist on the Earth's surface. All lines of latitude are parallel to one another. The circle around the centre of the Earth, midway between the **north pole** and the **south pole**, is called the Equator.

Lines of latitude are numbered in degrees from the Equator. The Equator is zero degrees (0°). The north pole is a point which is 90° North of the Equator. The south pole is 90° South of the Equator. All the other lines of latitude are numbered between 0° and 90°. The diagram below will help you remember whether a line is north or south of the Equator.

- Look at St Lucia on page 27. The island is at 14° of latitude. Is this 14°N or 14°S?

- Find a map of your country. Which lines of latitude pass through it? Are they north or south of the Equator? Write down the lines of latitude with °N or °S after the numbers.

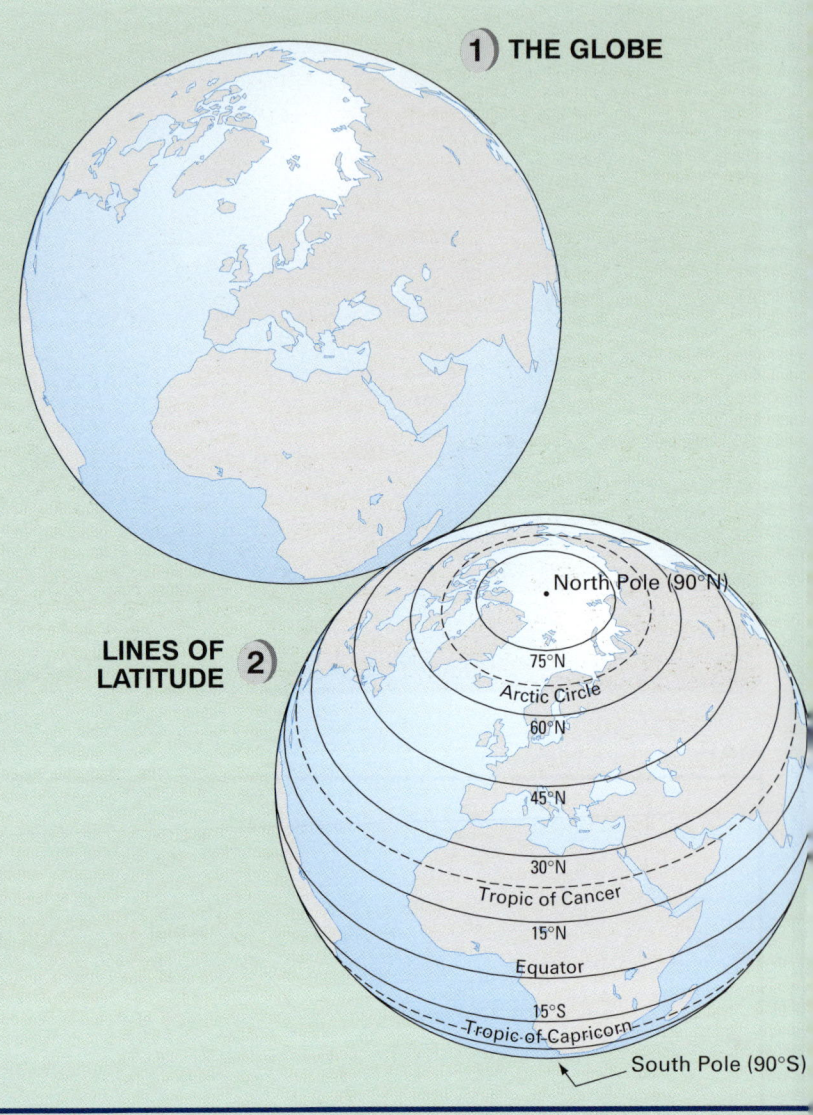

① THE GLOBE

② LINES OF LATITUDE

Reading latitude and longitude lines

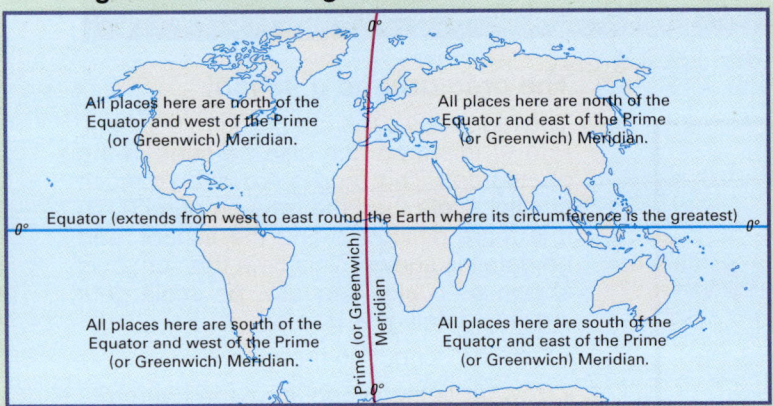

Different scales, different detail

Each of the three maps A, B and C takes up the same amount of space, but each shows a different area. This is because they each have a different scale. Map A has the largest scale; map C is the smallest scale map of the three. The area covered by Map A is highlighted on Maps B and C.

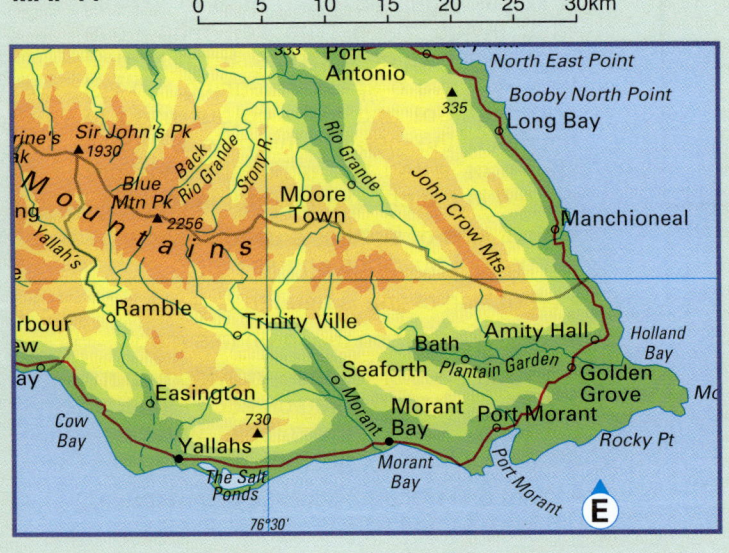

MAP A — Scale 1:600 000

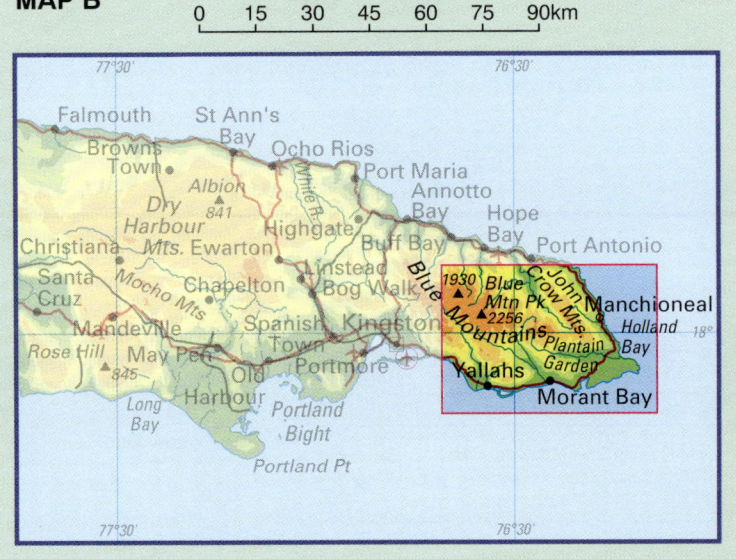

MAP B — Scale 1:2 000 000

Measuring Distance 5

LINES OF LATITUDE AND LONGITUDE 4

LINES OF LONGITUDE 3

Lines of longitude

Imaginary lines of **longitude** join the north and south poles. The line that passes through a place called Greenwich in London, England, (see page 48) is numbered 0°. This line of longitude is called the **prime meridian** or the **Greenwich meridian**.

On the opposite side of world from the prime meridian is the 180° line of longitude. All other lines are numbered between 0° west to 180°, and between 0° east to 180°. The diagram on page 4 will help you remember whether a line is east or west of the prime meridian.

The Caribbean region is west of the prime meridian, so all its lines of longitude are numbered West. For example on page 8, you can see lines 80°W and 75°W passing through Cuba.

- Find a map of your country. Which lines of longitude pass through it? Are they east or west of the prime meridian? Write down the lines of longitude with °E or °W after the numbers.

Calculating distance

The line scale on a map can be used to calculate the distance between two places. For example, how far is San Juan in Puerto Rico from Santo Domingo in the Dominican Republic? Find these places on page 9 of your atlas.

Use the straight edge of a piece of paper. Place it on the map, touching the symbols for both cities. Make a mark on your paper by Santo Domingo and then mark San Juan. Place your paper against the line scale. Put the mark for Santo Domingo beside 0 kilometres on the line scale. You will see the San Juan mark beside 400. The distance between the two cities is therefore 400 kilometres.

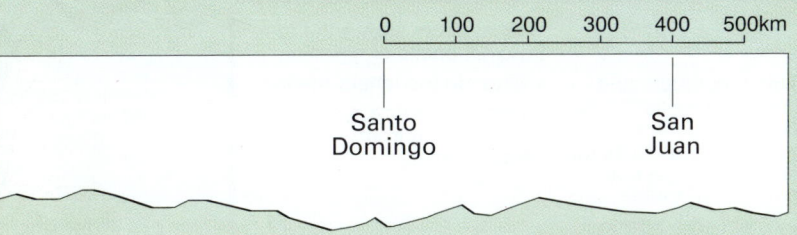

- Work out the distance between Kingston, Jamaica, and Port of Spain, Trinidad, from the map on pages 8 to 9.

- What happens to the detail shown on Map A when the scale gets smaller (compare Map A with highlighted areas on Maps B and C)?

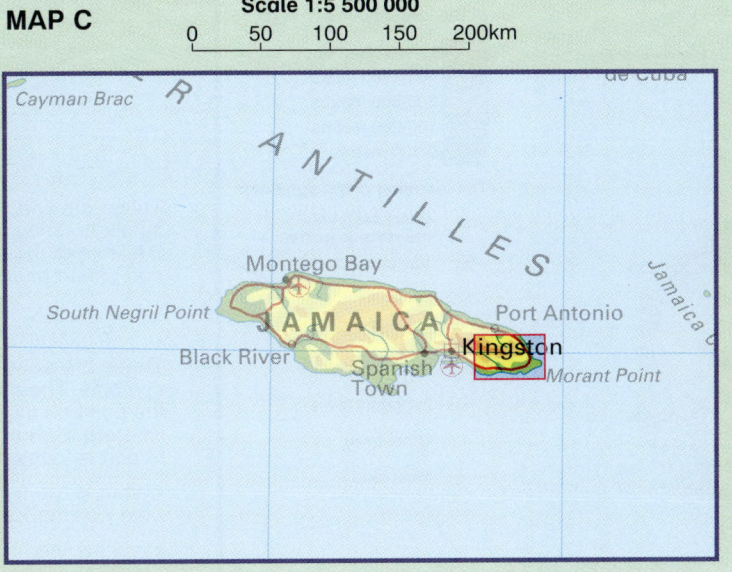

MAP C Scale 1:5 500 000

© Bartholomew Ltd.

6 Using this Atlas

How your Caribbean School Atlas is organised

Your atlas is organised in five parts. Pages 1 to 7 introduce you to key skills in using the atlas. Each map in your atlas has a scale, a key, and the cardinal points. Pages 8 to 45 has maps of all the Caribbean territories. The order that countries appear is from the west (Belize) to the south east (Guyana).

Pages 47 to 61 have a set of two maps for six of the continents, one map showing the continent's **landscape** or **relief** features, the other showing how it is divided into **countries**. The continent of **Antarctica** is shown on the World maps on pages 46 to 49. There are **thematic maps** of the world in the fourth part of the atlas, pages 50 to 69, covering important issues such as threats to the environment.

At the end of the atlas is an **index** to important place names and topics.

- Study the list of contents on the inside of the front cover. This list makes it easy for you to find the map you want.
- Go to page 71. Study how to find a place you look up in the index. Find Tokyo on a map using the information in the index.

Alongside this atlas, you may use the Caribbean School Atlas Skills Workbook. The workbook provides exercises to build up your map skills.

Landscape maps for Caribbean countries

There is a Landscape map for every Caribbean country like Example A below. Read the notes and answer the questions around the map of St Kitts and Nevis. These will help you understand all the elements of a Landscape map.

Relief maps of the six continents use colours to show the height of the land, just as the Caribbean Landscape maps. But the keys are different. It is essential that you use a map's key to interpret lines, symbols and colours. The key varies from map to map.

Using the St Kitts and Nevis' map and its key, below, answer these practice questions:
- What do these lines represent?
- What is found where these symbols are shown?
- What do these colours represent?
- What do the same colours represent on the Relief map of Africa on page 58?
- How many minutes is a degree divided into?

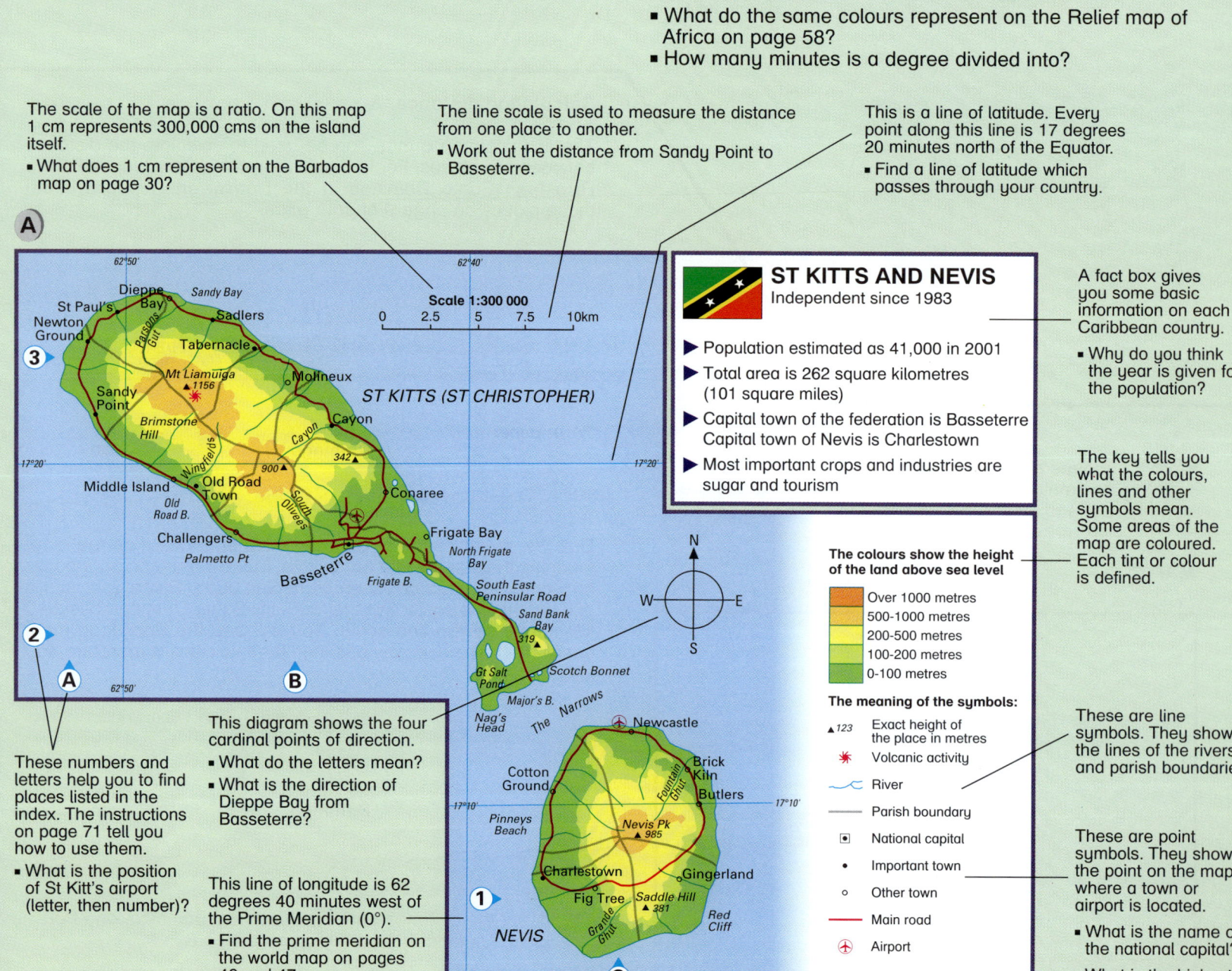

Political divisions

Continents are divided into countries. Countries are divided into smaller administrative units. Maps for the Caribbean, and for each of the continents, show these kinds of divisions. Colours used to tint **political divisions** have no meaning; they are only used to clearly distinguish the different areas. For this reason such maps do not have a key. The land areas shaded grey on a map of a continent are places not regarded as a part of that continent.

The atlas has maps of the internal political or administrative divisions of Caribbean countries. The divisions may be called regions, parishes, counties or districts, according to the country. These are distinguished by shades of brown, red or pink. The shades have no meaning.

- How many countries are there in South America?
- What are the grey areas on the map of South America?
- How many districts is St Lucia divided into?

Thematic maps, graphs and diagrams

These are special maps designed to show one topic or theme. Example B is a **thematic map** of Barbados that shows the areas that are settlements. The grey areas on the map are agricultural or not utilised. The **Resources** maps of the Caribbean section are also thematic maps. These maps show the ways that a country is productive: the crops farmers grow, the products made in factories, and the minerals extracted from the ground.

Different kinds of graph are also used. Example C is a **pie graph**, which shows the parts of the total population of Trinidad and Tobago, according to the place their ancestors came from. Example D uses a **line graph** to show temperature patterns in Kingston, and a **bar graph** to show the pattern of Kingston's rainfall over the twelve months of the year. Example E is also a bar graph. Each bar shows a different product.

Diagrams are also used in the atlas to present complicated information in a way that you can understand more easily. An example of a diagram is the box showing the official languages of countries of the Caribbean on page 8.

- Look through the atlas and find five kinds of thematic maps.
- What does the graph below showing Kingston's rainfall tell you?
- Find another bar graph in the atlas. What does it tell you?
- What does the diagram on page 20 tell you about the islands of the Eastern Caribbean?

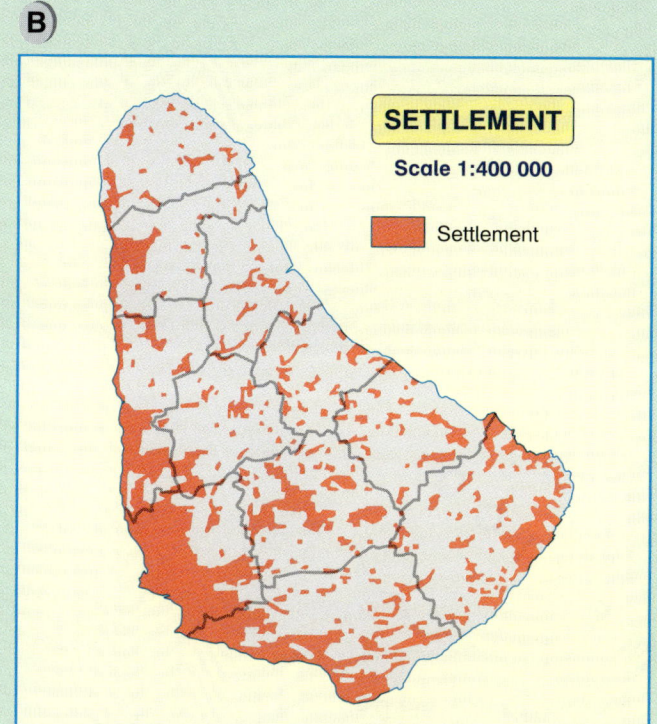

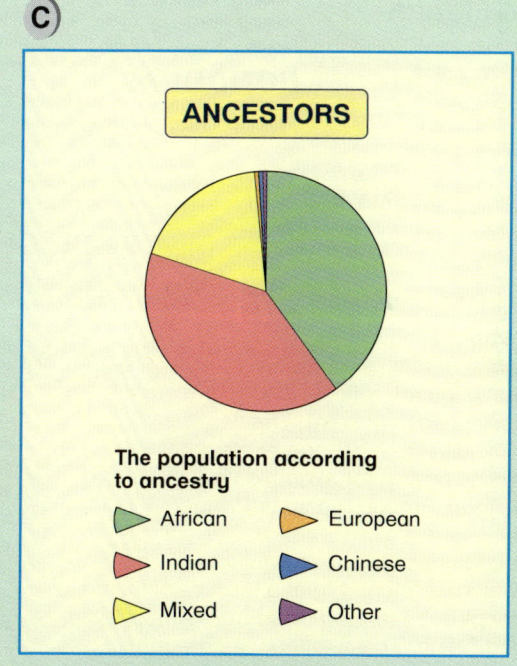

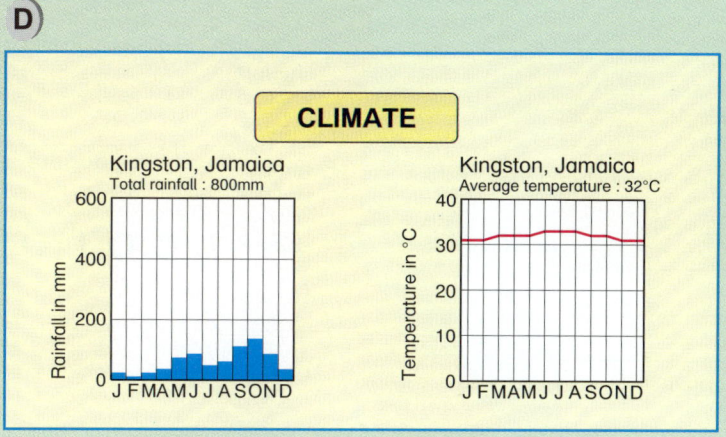

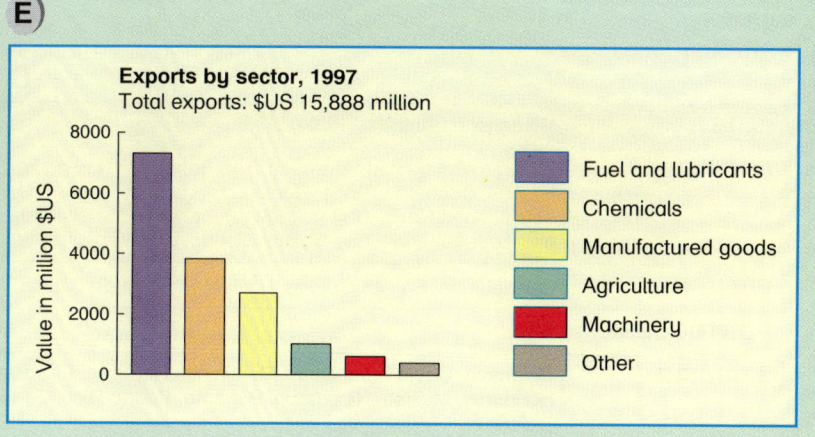

8 Caribbean : Countries, Languages

Languages in the Caribbean

The diagram below shows the official language of each country on this map. The language reflects the colonial history of each country. The language is usually the language of the most recent colonising power, for example United Kingdom, Holland, France, Spain or Portugal.

Many of the countries also have unofficial Creole languages which developed from a mixture of the various immigrant peoples, especially those from Africa, India, Indonesia and China. These languages are the popular languages of the Caribbean countries and are used in song, theatre, politics and everyday life.

- What is the official language of your country?
- Are other languages also used?

DUTCH	Netherlands Antilles, Aruba, Suriname
ENGLISH	Anguilla, Antigua and Barbuda, The Bahamas, Barbados, Belize, British Virgin Islands, Cayman Islands, Dominica, Grenada, Guyana, Jamaica, St Kitts and Nevis, St Lucia, St Vincent and the Grenadines, Trinidad and Tobago, Turks and Caicos Islands, U.S. Virgin Islands
FRENCH	Guadeloupe, French Guiana, Haiti, Martinique, St Martin
PORTUGUESE	Brazil
SPANISH	Colombia, Costa Rica, Cuba, Dominican Republic, El Salvador, Guatemala, Honduras, Mexico, Nicaragua, Panama, Puerto Rico, Venezuela

The Caribbean Community

Fifteen countries of the Caribbean have joined in an association called The Caribbean Community, or CARICOM, to foster trade and cooperation in many areas. These countries and their flags are shown on the back cover.

- In what ways do the members of CARICOM cooperate?

The Prime Ministers of CARICOM countries meet once a year to cooperate on matters concerning the Caribbean region. These Prime Ministers participated in the 1999 meeting in Trinidad and Tobago.

Cities and towns
- ⊡ Capital cities
- • Important towns

Scale 1:10 500 000
0 100 200 300 400 500km

© Bartholomew Ltd.

10 Greater Antilles : The Bahamas

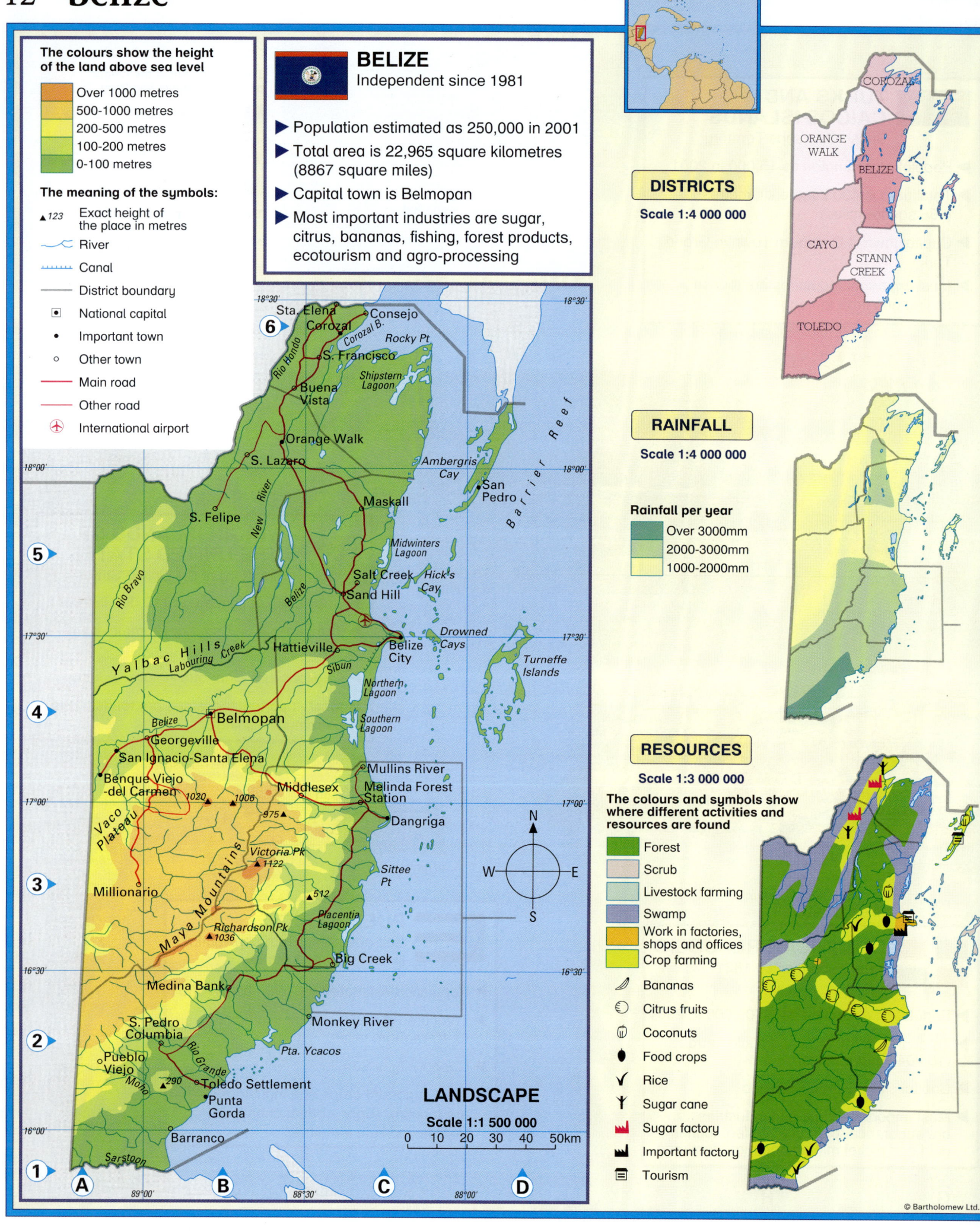

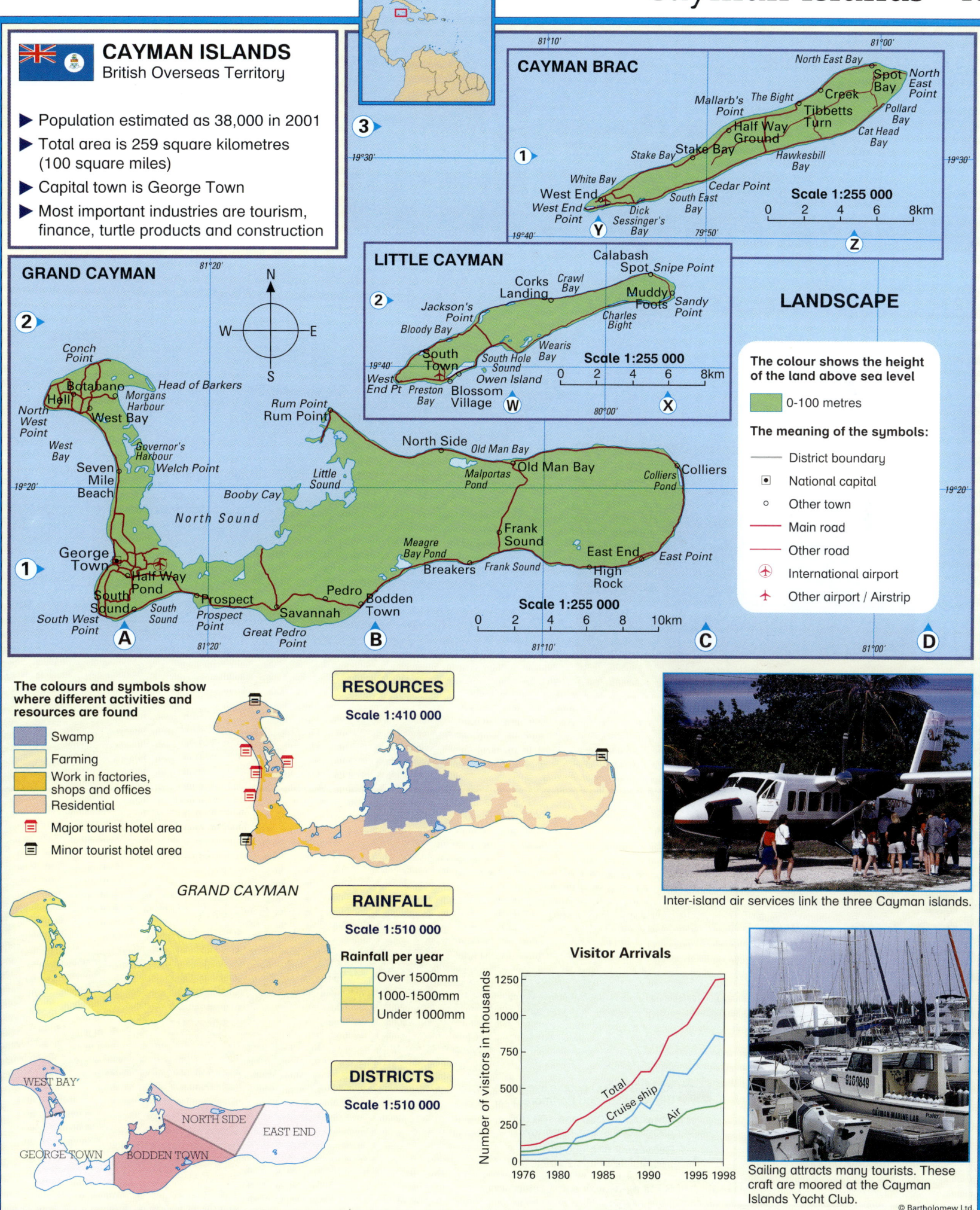

Jamaica : Landscape : People

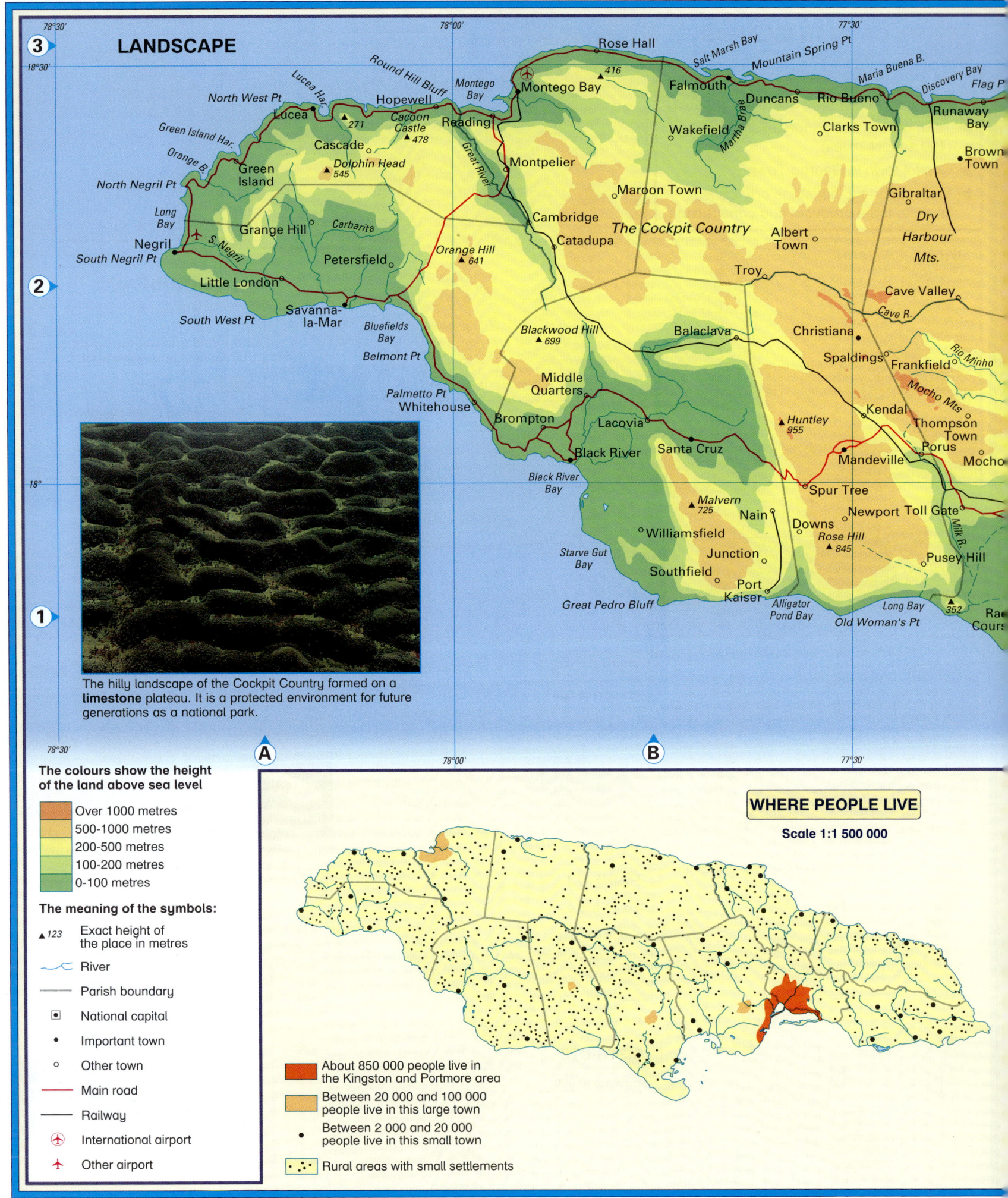

The hilly landscape of the Cockpit Country formed on a **limestone** plateau. It is a protected environment for future generations as a national park.

LANDSCAPE

The colours show the height of the land above sea level
- Over 1000 metres
- 500–1000 metres
- 200–500 metres
- 100–200 metres
- 0–100 metres

The meaning of the symbols:
- ▲123 Exact height of the place in metres
- River
- Parish boundary
- ▣ National capital
- • Important town
- ○ Other town
- Main road
- Railway
- ✈ International airport
- ✈ Other airport

WHERE PEOPLE LIVE
Scale 1:1 500 000

- About 850 000 people live in the Kingston and Portmore area
- Between 20 000 and 100 000 people live in this large town
- Between 2 000 and 20 000 people live in this small town
- Rural areas with small settlements

16 Jamaica Climate : Tourism

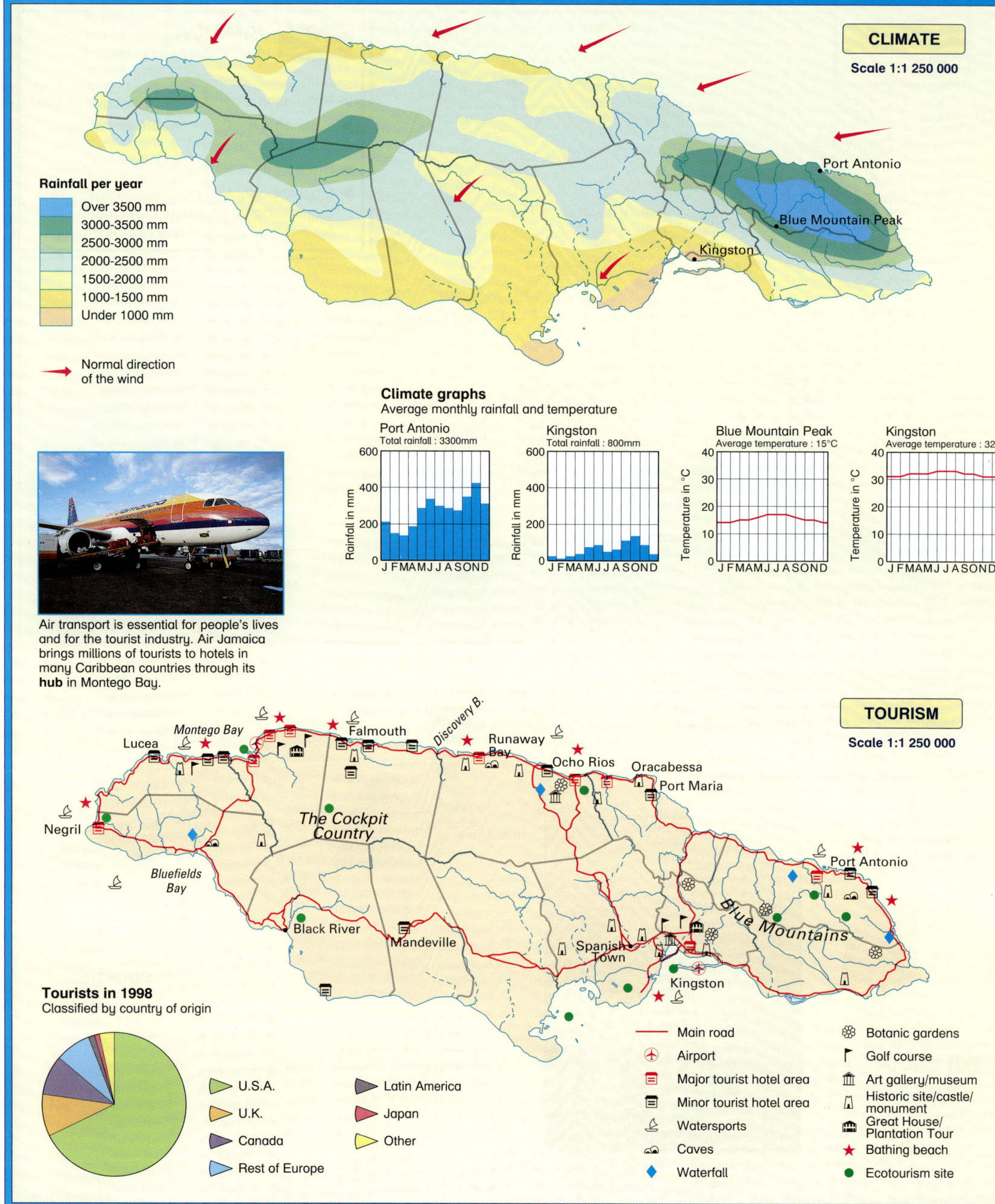

Resources 17

AGRICULTURE
Scale 1:1 250 000

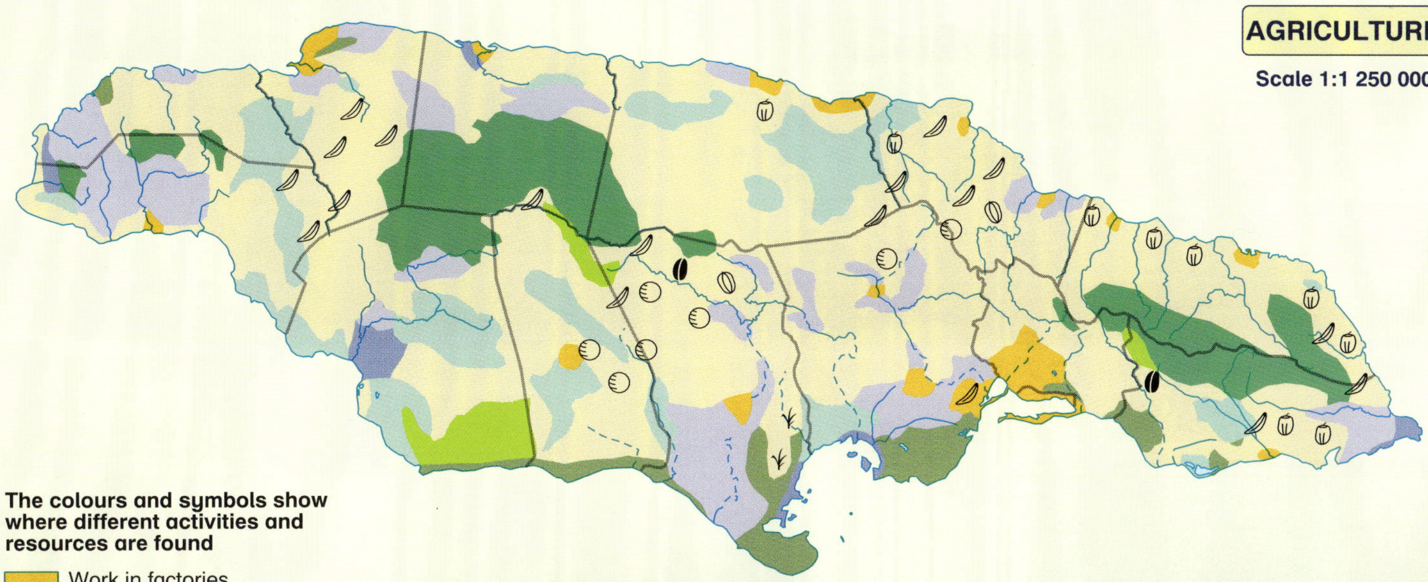

The colours and symbols show where different activities and resources are found

- Work in factories, shops and offices
- Rain forest
- Dry scrub forest
- Morass and swamp
- Livestock farming
- Sugar cane
- Small mixed cultivations
- Intensive vegetable growing
- Coconuts
- Bananas
- Citrus fruits
- Cocoa
- Coffee
- Sisal

Small scale farmers in southern Trelawny harvest yellow yams. These are exported to North America.

Bauxite mined in Jamaica is refined into alumina at several large factories like this one at Kirkvine, in Manchester. The alumina is shipped to other countries to make aluminium.

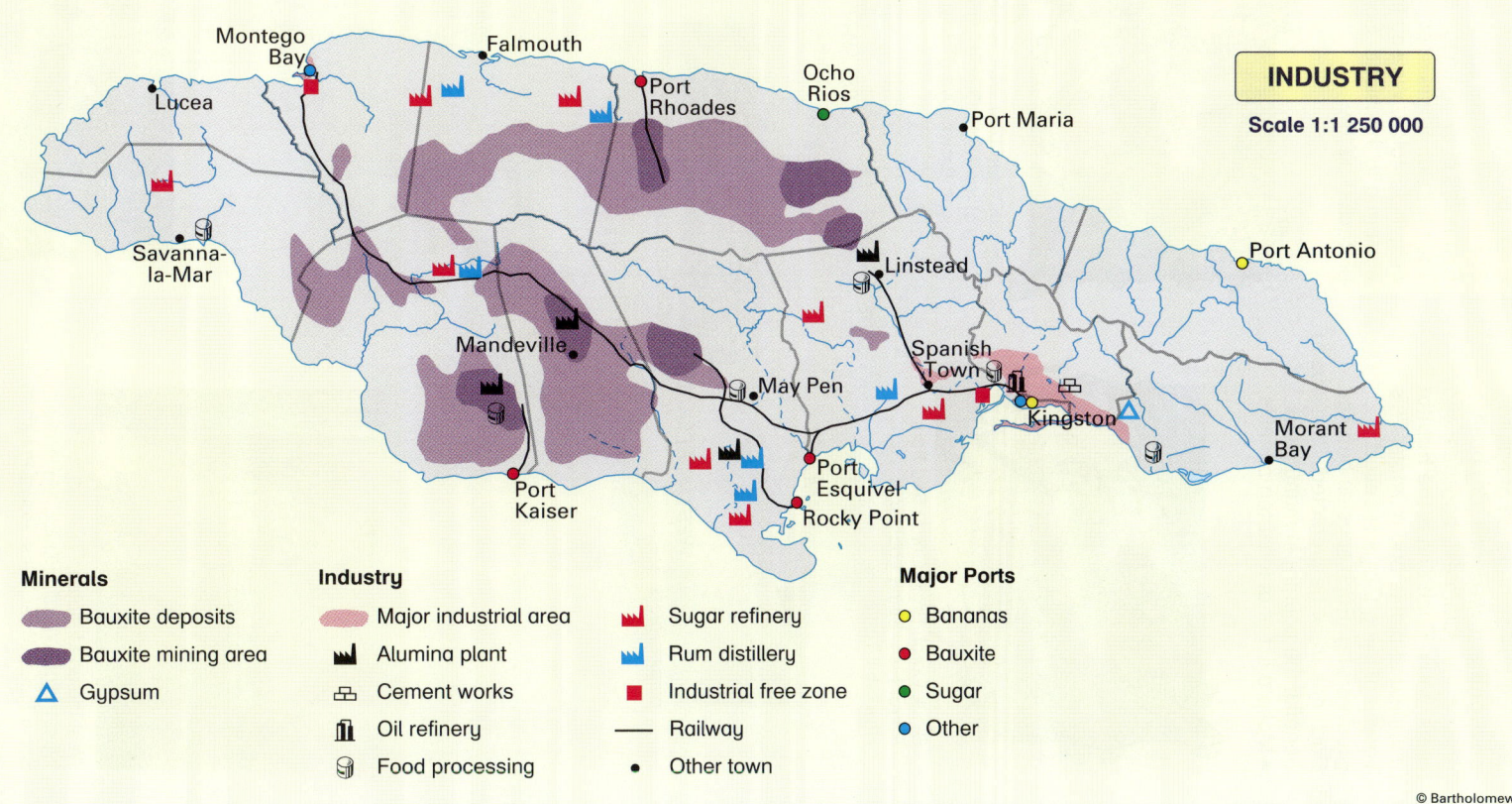

INDUSTRY
Scale 1:1 250 000

Minerals
- Bauxite deposits
- Bauxite mining area
- Gypsum

Industry
- Major industrial area
- Alumina plant
- Cement works
- Oil refinery
- Food processing
- Sugar refinery
- Rum distillery
- Industrial free zone
- Railway
- Other town

Major Ports
- Bananas
- Bauxite
- Sugar
- Other

© Bartholomew Ltd.

18 Jamaica : Biodiversity

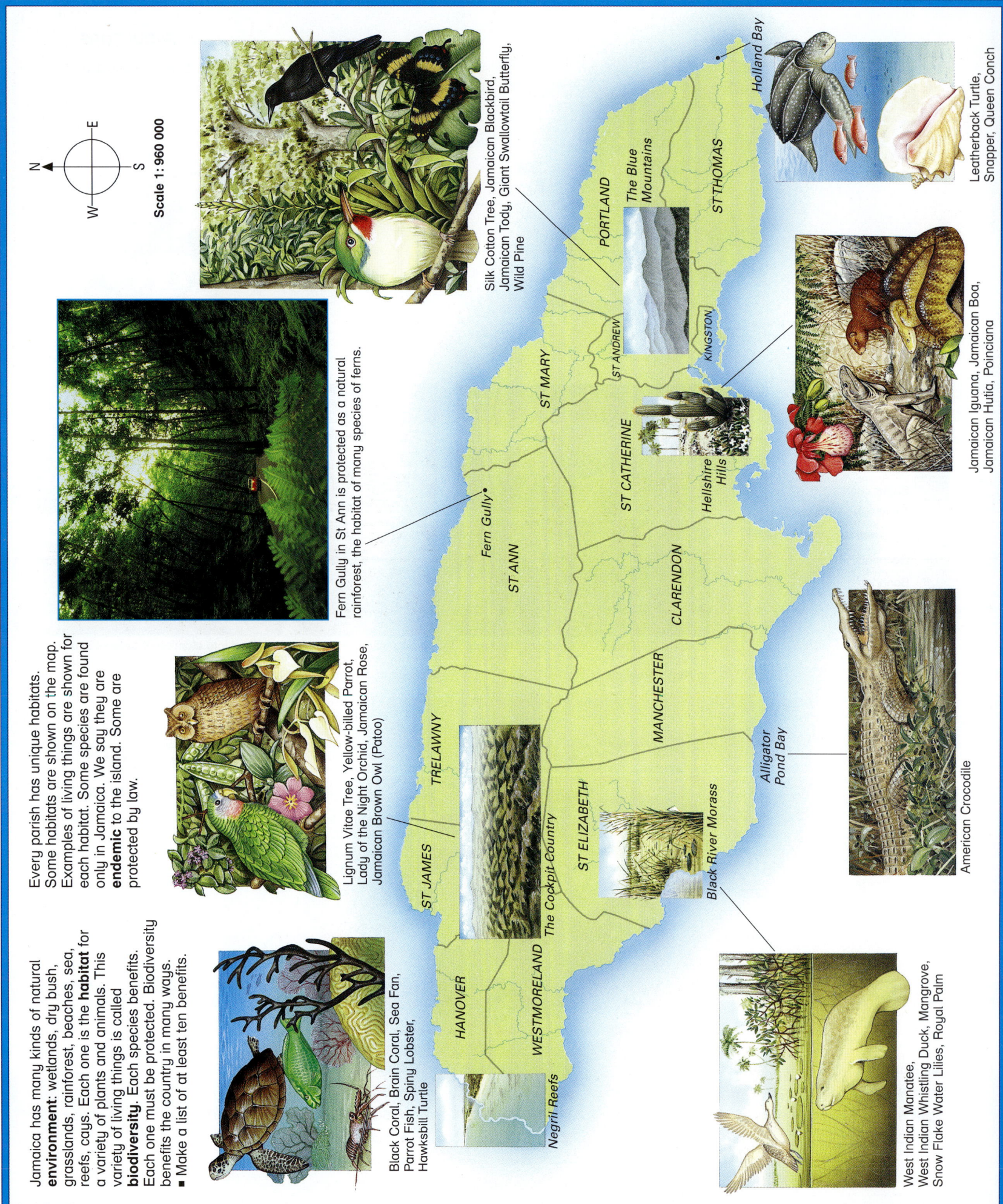

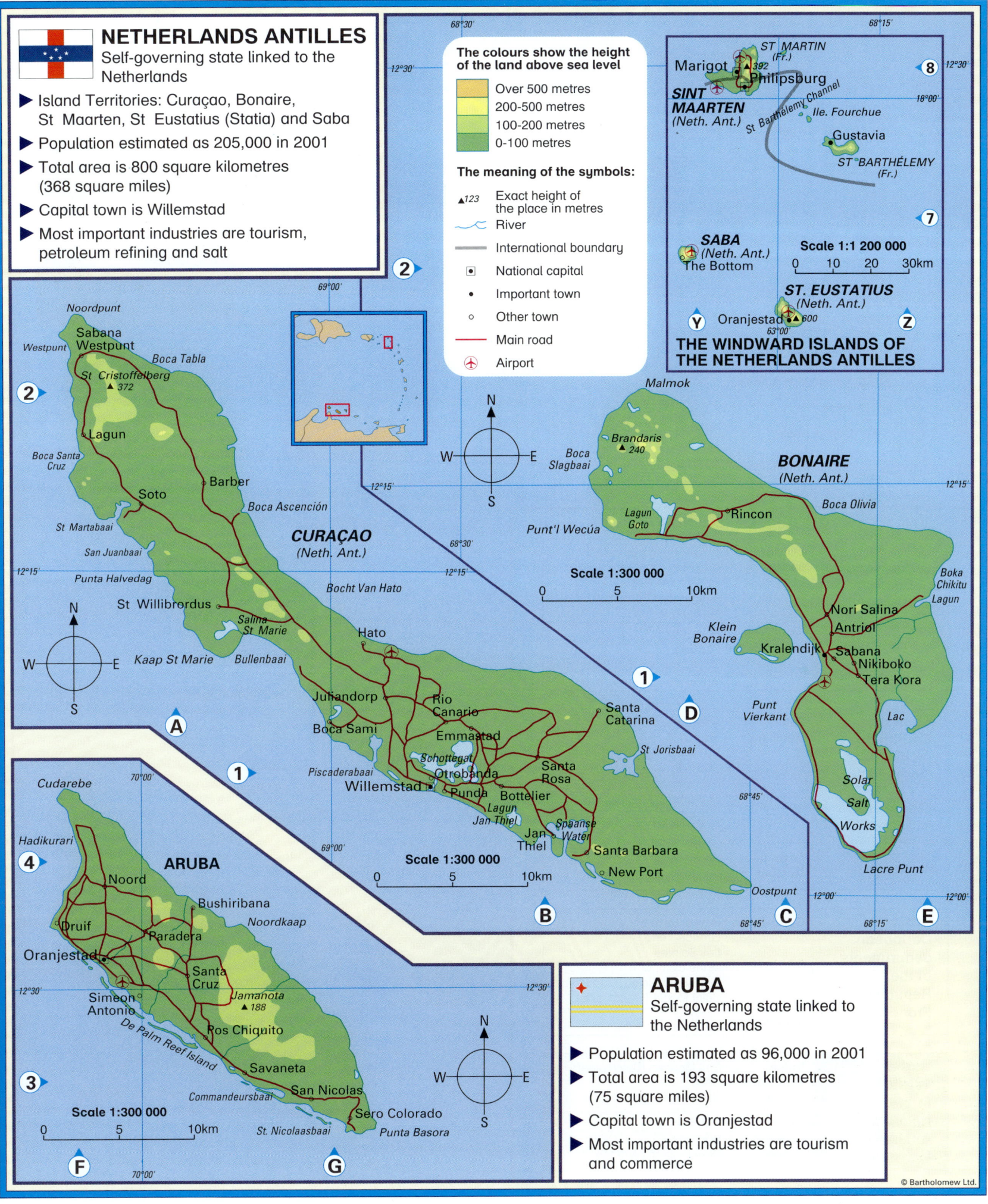

Eastern Caribbean

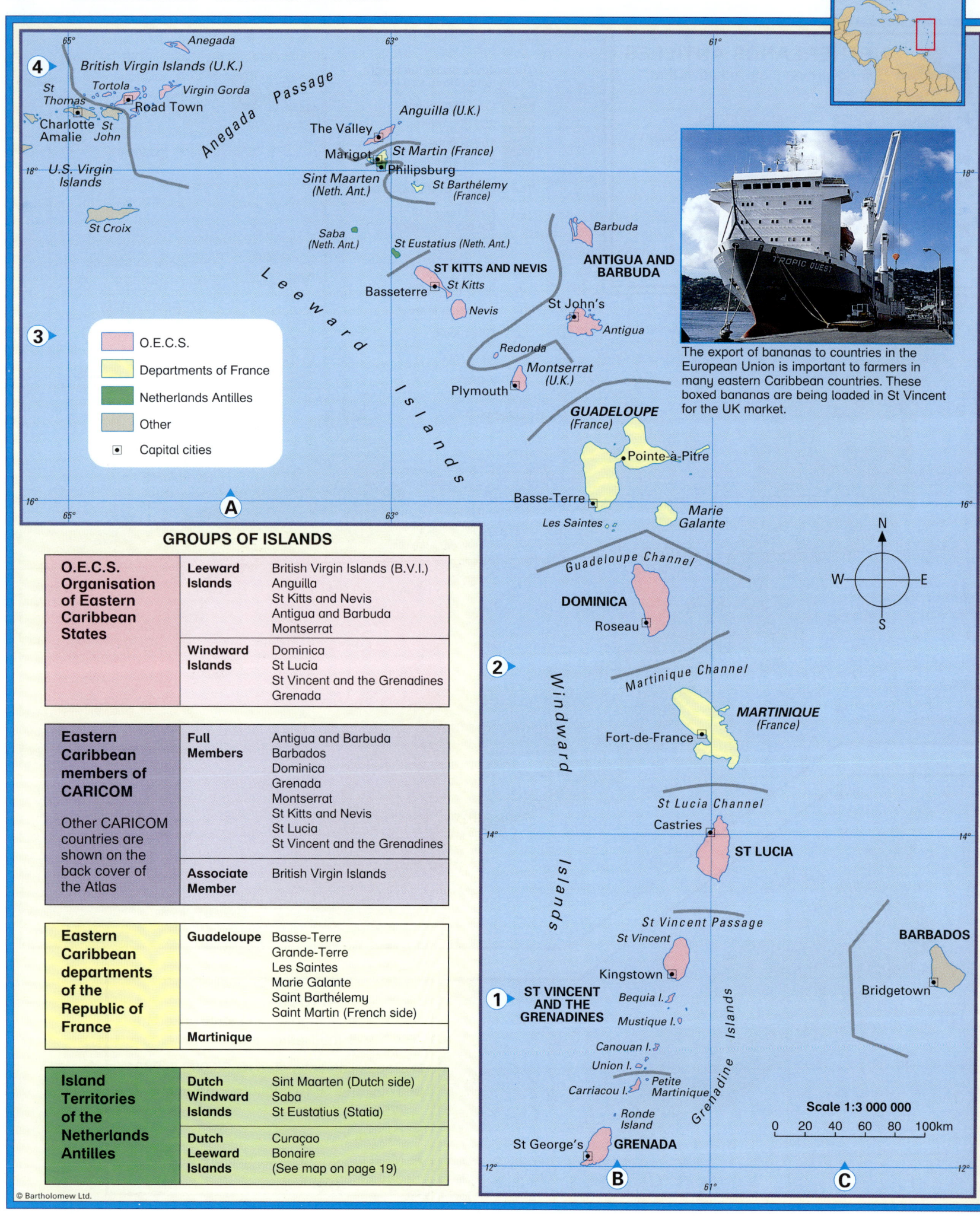

The export of bananas to countries in the European Union is important to farmers in many eastern Caribbean countries. These boxed bananas are being loaded in St Vincent for the UK market.

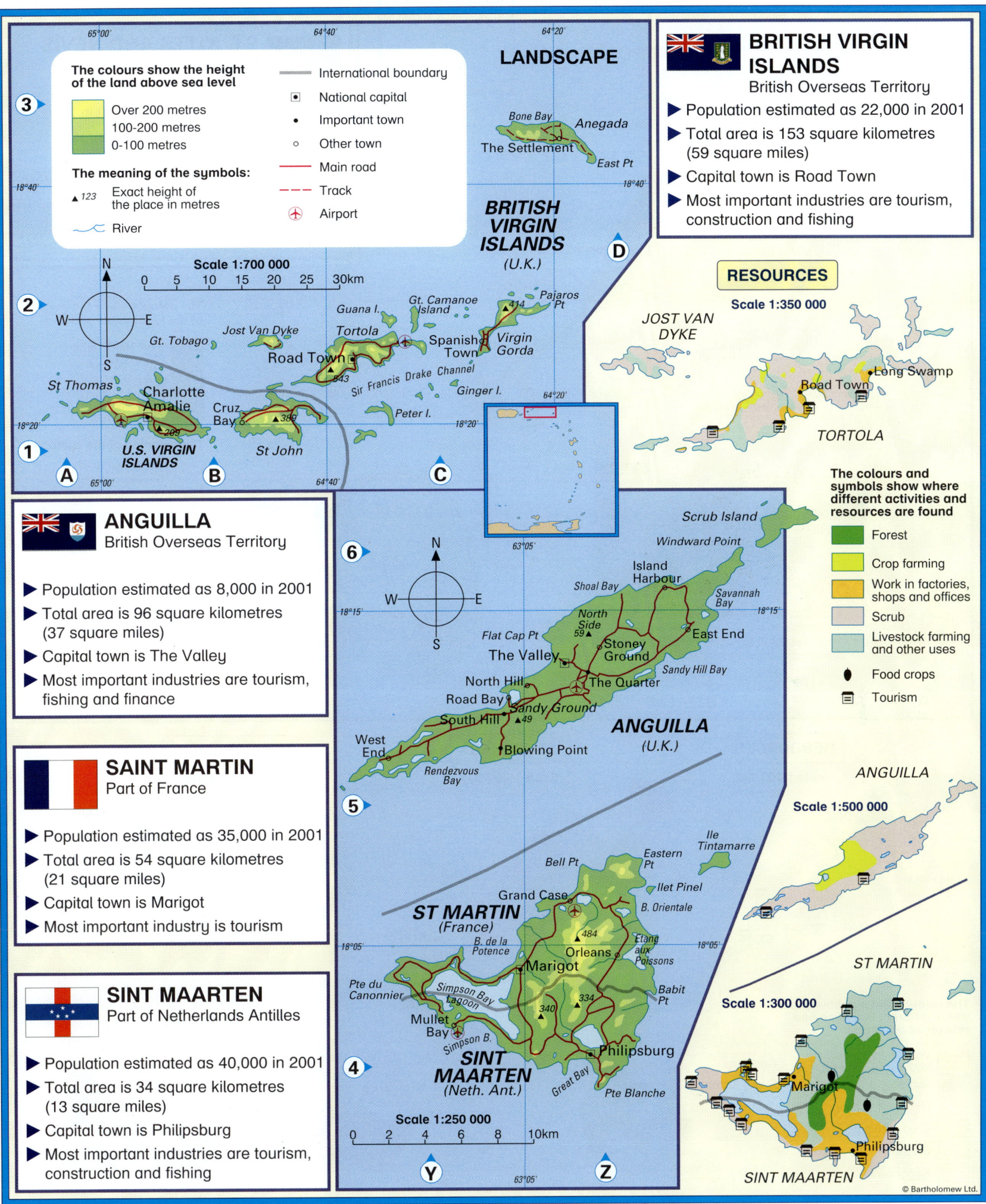

St Kitts and Nevis

ST KITTS AND NEVIS
Independent since 1983

- Population estimated as 41,000 in 2001
- Total area is 262 square kilometres (101 square miles)
- Capital town of the federation is Basseterre. Capital town of Nevis is Charlestown
- Most important crops and industries are sugar and tourism

LANDSCAPE

Scale 1:250 000

St Kitts (St Christopher) features: Dieppe Bay, St Paul's, Newton Ground, Sandy Bay, Sadlers, Parsons Gut, Tabernacle, Mt Liamuiga 1156, Molineux, Sandy Point, Brimstone Hill, Cayon, Wingfields, 342, Middle Island, Old Road Town, 900, South Olivees, Old Road B., Conaree, Challengers, Palmetto Pt, Basseterre, Frigate Bay, North Frigate Bay, Frigate B., South East Peninsular Road, Sand Bank Bay, 319, Gt Salt Pond, Scotch Bonnet, Major's B., Nag's Head, The Narrows.

Nevis features: Newcastle, Cotton Ground, Brick Kiln, Butlers, Fountain Ghut, Pinneys Beach, Nevis Pk 985, Charlestown, Gingerland, Fig Tree, Saddle Hill 381, Grande Ghut, Red Cliff.

The fortress at Brimstone Hill in St. Kitts was built to defend the island, captured by the English, from French invaders. Tourists learn about the Caribbean by visiting historical sites.

The colours show the height of the land above sea level
- Over 1000 metres
- 500-1000 metres
- 200-500 metres
- 100-200 metres
- 0-100 metres

The meaning of the symbols:
- ▲123 Exact height of the place in metres
- ✹ Volcanic activity
- River
- Parish boundary
- ⊡ National capital
- • Important town
- ○ Other town
- — Main road
- ✈ Airport

RESOURCES
Scale 1:400 000

The colours and symbols show where different activities and resources are found

- Work in factories, shops and offices
- Forest
- Livestock farming
- Crop farming
- Scrub
- Sugar cane
- Coconuts
- Sugar factory
- Tourism

PARISHES
Scale 1:400 000

St Kitts: ST PAUL'S, ST JOHN, ST ANNE, CHRIST CHURCH, ST MARY, ST THOMAS, ST PETER, TRINITY, ST GEORGE

Nevis: ST JAMES, ST THOMAS, ST PAUL, ST JOHN, ST GEORGE

RAINFALL
Scale 1:400 000

Rainfall per year
- Over 3000mm
- 2000-3000mm
- 1000-2000mm
- 0-1000mm

© Bartholomew Ltd.

Montserrat 23

MONTSERRAT
British Overseas Territory

- Population estimated as 4,000 in 2001
- Total area is 102 square kilometres (39 square miles)
- Plymouth, the former capital, has been abandoned
- Construction is the most important activity

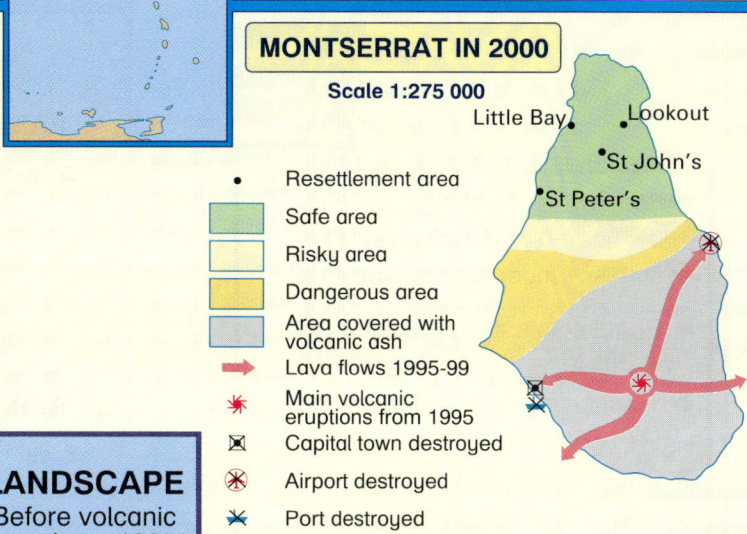

MONTSERRAT IN 2000
Scale 1:275 000

Symbols:
- Resettlement area
- Safe area
- Risky area
- Dangerous area
- Area covered with volcanic ash
- Lava flows 1995-99
- Main volcanic eruptions from 1995
- Capital town destroyed
- Airport destroyed
- Port destroyed

Safe Zone
In 2000, 4000 Montserratians were left on the island. 6000 had moved to other countries. Those who remained were living in the northern third of the island. New homes, schools, hotels and a new port were under construction.

Exclusion Zone
Everyone was evacuated from the centre and south of Montserrat. All homes, hotels, schools, offices, ports and farms were destroyed or buried in ash. The volcano was still active in 2000.

CROSS SECTION OF A VOLCANO

Montserrat's long dormant volcanoes erupted between 1995 and 2000. Two-thirds of the island was covered with lava and ash. The shape of the coastline was changed. The capital, Plymouth, was buried. The airport was destroyed. People moved to the north of the island.

The main street in Plymouth under several metres of volcanic material in 1999.

LANDSCAPE
Before volcanic eruptions, 1995

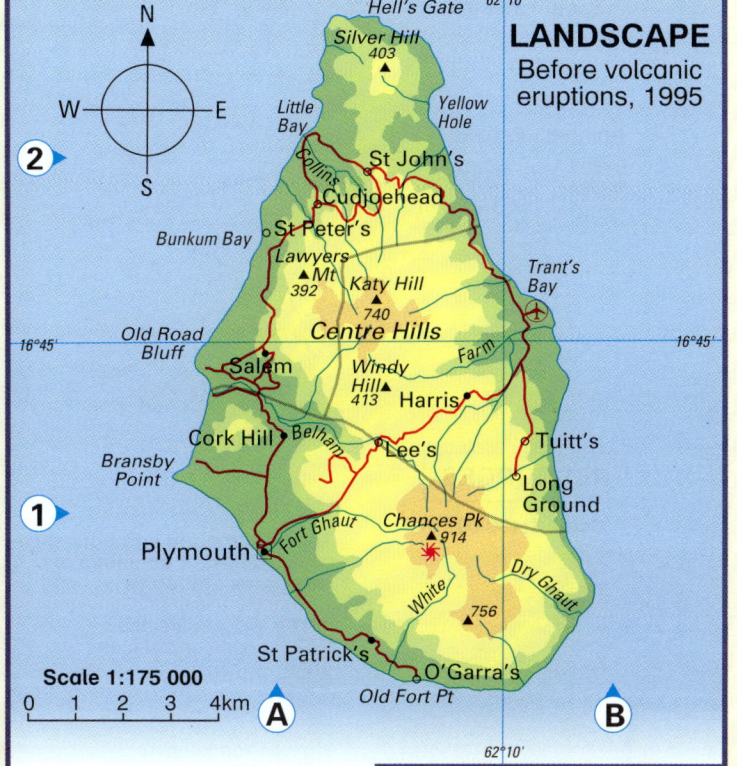

Scale 1:175 000

The colours show the height of the land above sea level
- Over 500 metres
- 200-500 metres
- 100-200 metres
- 0-100 metres

The meaning of the symbols:
- ▲123 Exact height of the place in metres
- Volcanic activity
- River
- Parish boundary
- Former capital town
- Important town
- Other town
- Main road
- International airport

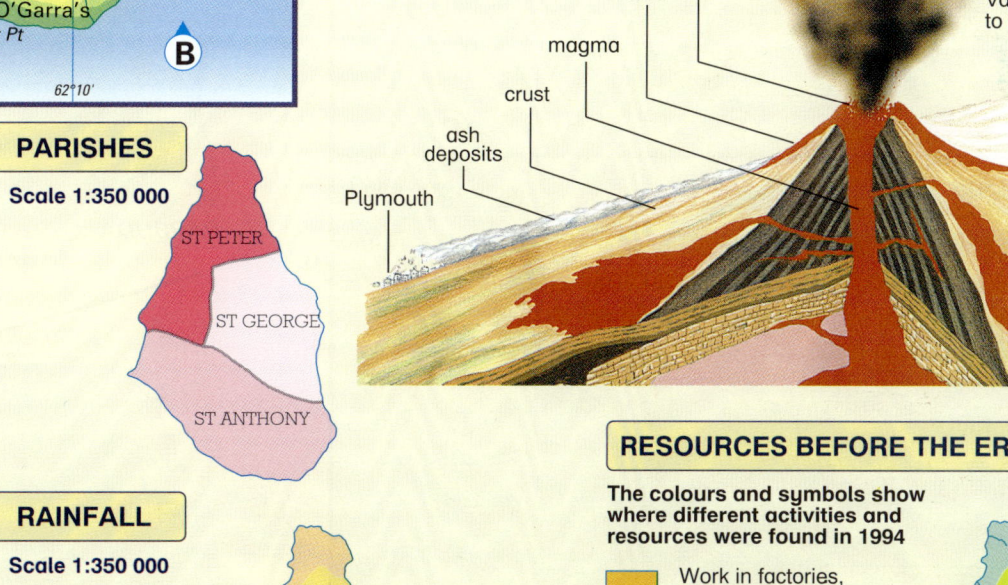

Labels: crater, lava, magma, crust, ash deposits, Plymouth. Vapour billows up to 20,000 metres.

PARISHES
Scale 1:350 000

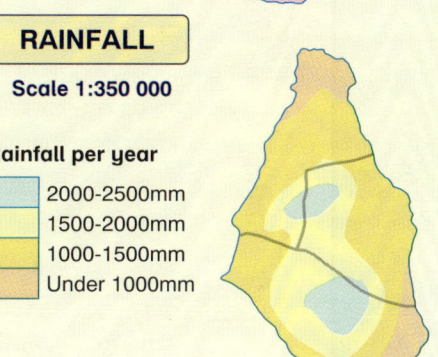

ST PETER, ST GEORGE, ST ANTHONY

RAINFALL
Scale 1:350 000

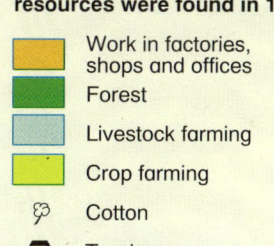

Rainfall per year
- 2000-2500mm
- 1500-2000mm
- 1000-1500mm
- Under 1000mm

RESOURCES BEFORE THE ERUPTIONS

The colours and symbols show where different activities and resources were found in 1994

- Work in factories, shops and offices
- Forest
- Livestock farming
- Crop farming
- Cotton
- Tourism

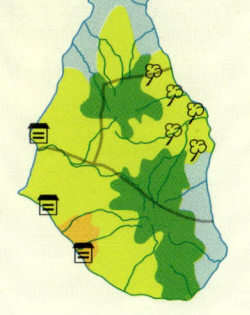

Scale 1:350 000

© Bartholomew Ltd.

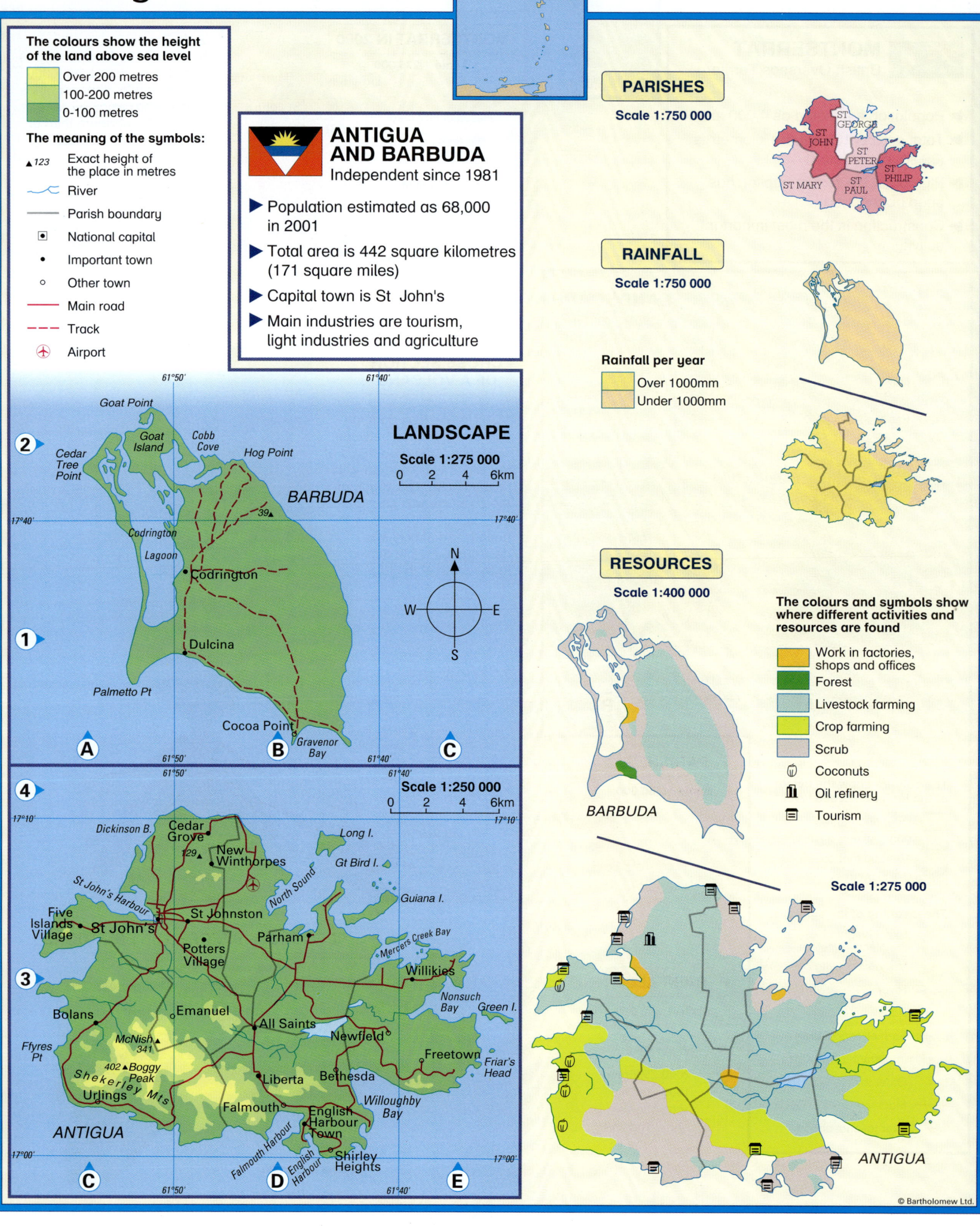

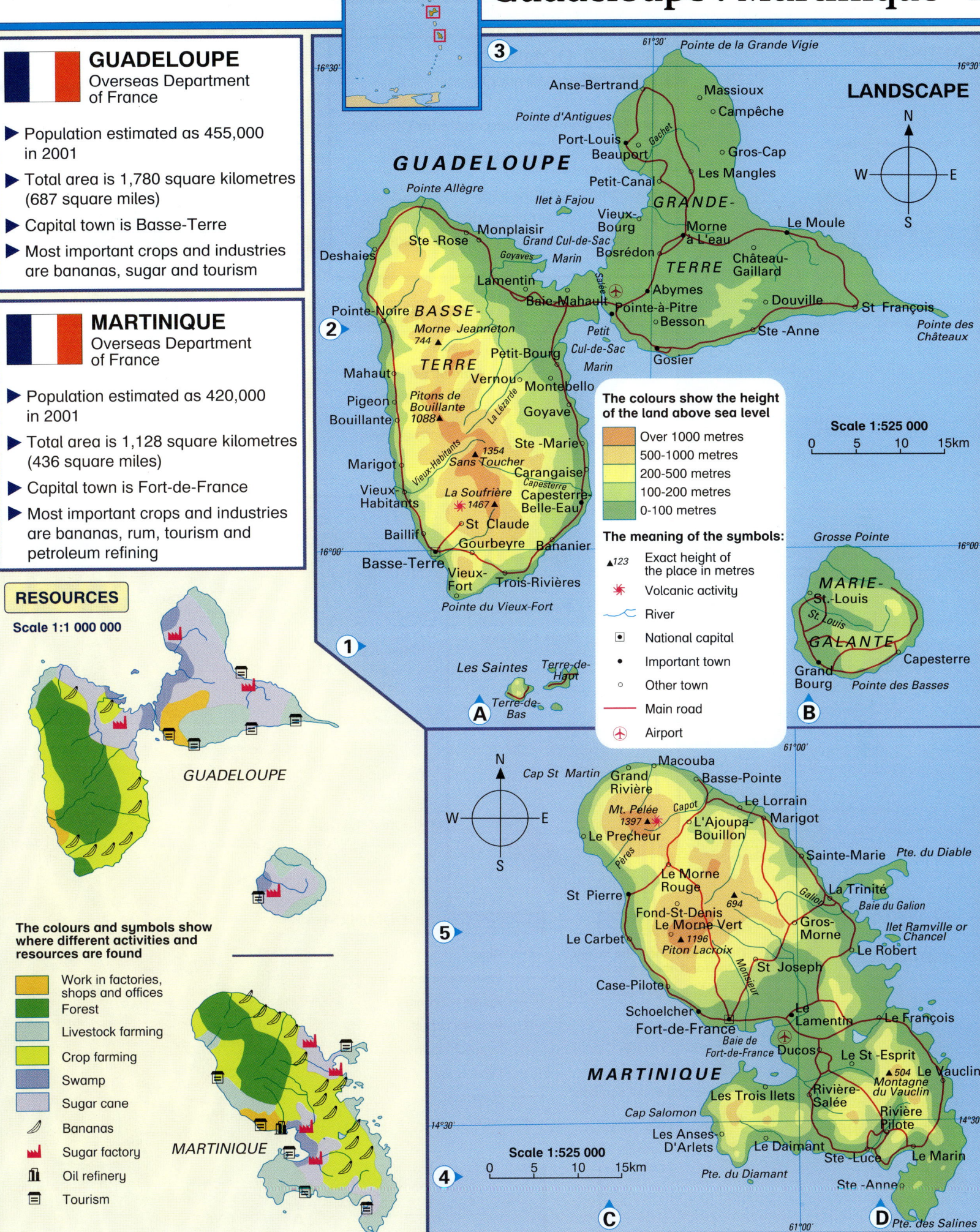

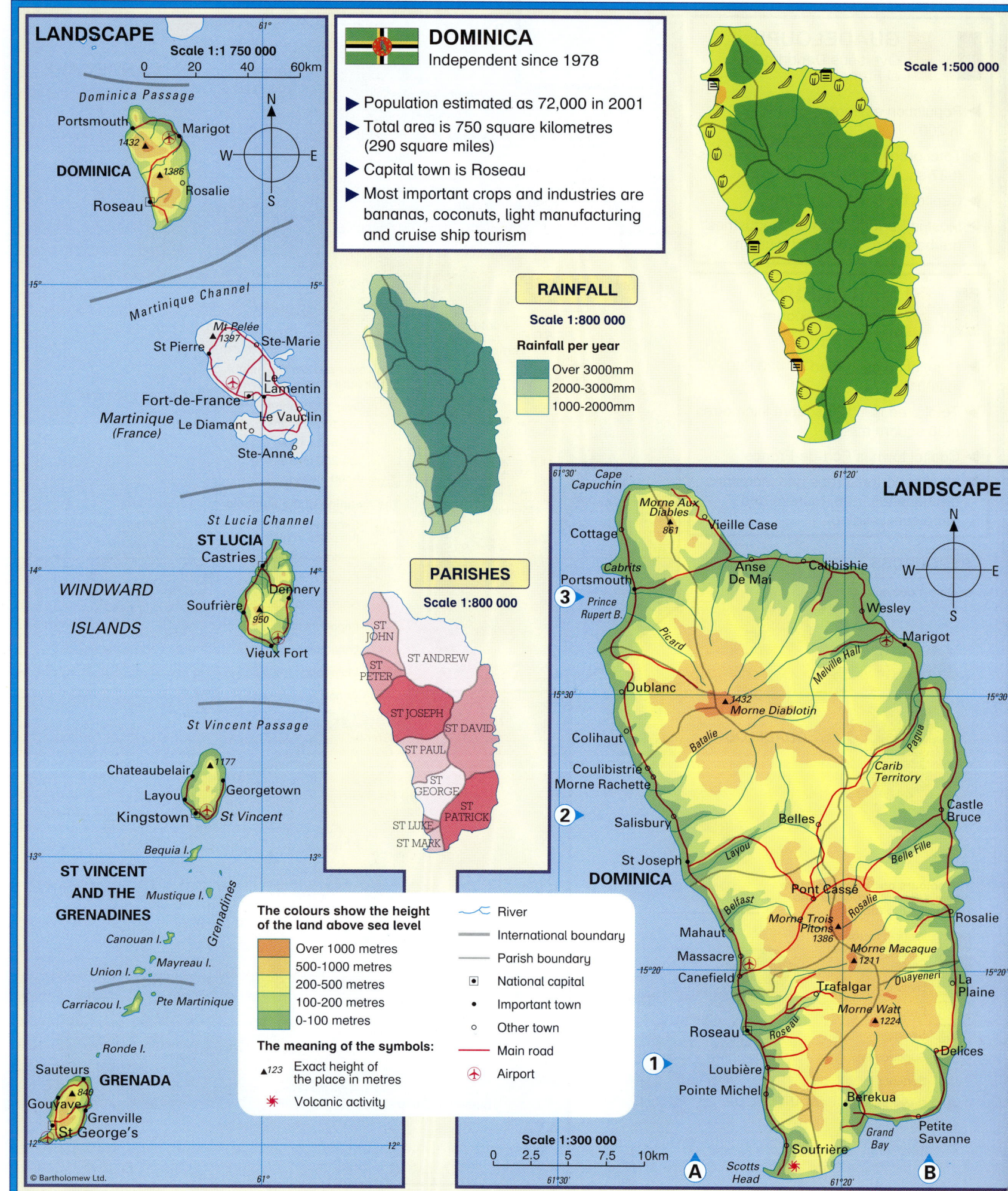

St Lucia

ST LUCIA
Independent since 1979

- Population estimated as 150,000 in 2001
- Total area is 616 square kilometres (238 square miles)
- Capital town is Castries
- Most important crops and industries are tourism, bananas, coconuts, cocoa and light industries

RESOURCES
Scale 1:400 000

The colours and symbols show where different activities and resources are found

- Work in factories, shops and offices
- Forest
- Livestock farming
- Crop farming

Symbols:
- Coconuts
- Bananas
- Citrus fruits
- Cocoa
- Important factories
- Tourism
- Oil terminal

RAINFALL
Scale 1:800 000

Rainfall per year:
- Over 3000mm
- 2000-3000mm
- 1000-2000mm

DISTRICTS
Scale 1:800 000

Districts: Gros Islet, Dauphin, Castries, Anse La Raye, Dennery, Soufrière, Praslin, Micoud, Choiseul, Laborie, Vieux Fort

LANDSCAPE
Scale 1:250 000

The colours show the height of the land above sea level:
- Over 1000 metres
- 500-1000 metres
- 200-500 metres
- 100-200 metres
- 0-100 metres

The meaning of the symbols:
- ▲123 Exact height of the place in metres
- Volcanic activity
- River
- District boundary
- National capital
- Important town
- Other town
- Main road
- Airport

Places on landscape map: Pte du Cap, Pigeon Pt, Rodney Bay, Gros Islet, Anse Lavoutte, Bon Terre, Monchy, Cape Marquis, Choc Bay, Mt Chaubourg 352, Marquis, Port Castries, Vigie, Castries, Babonneau, Grande Anse Bay, The Mourne, Ciceron, La Sorcière 675, Marigot, La Croix Maingot, Bexon, Cul de Sac, Roseau, Anse la Raye, Grande Rivière, Louvet, Mabouya, Canaries, Dennery, Mt Gimie 950, Praslin, Soufrière, Petit Piton 750, Fond St Jacques, Mon Repos, Gros Piton 798, Fond, Troumassée, Anse L'Ivrogne, Desruisseaux, Micoud, Canelles, Vieux Fort, Choiseul, Augier, Saltibus Pt., Laborie, Vieux Fort, Hewanorra, Maria Islands, Vieux Fort Bay, Cape Moule à Chique

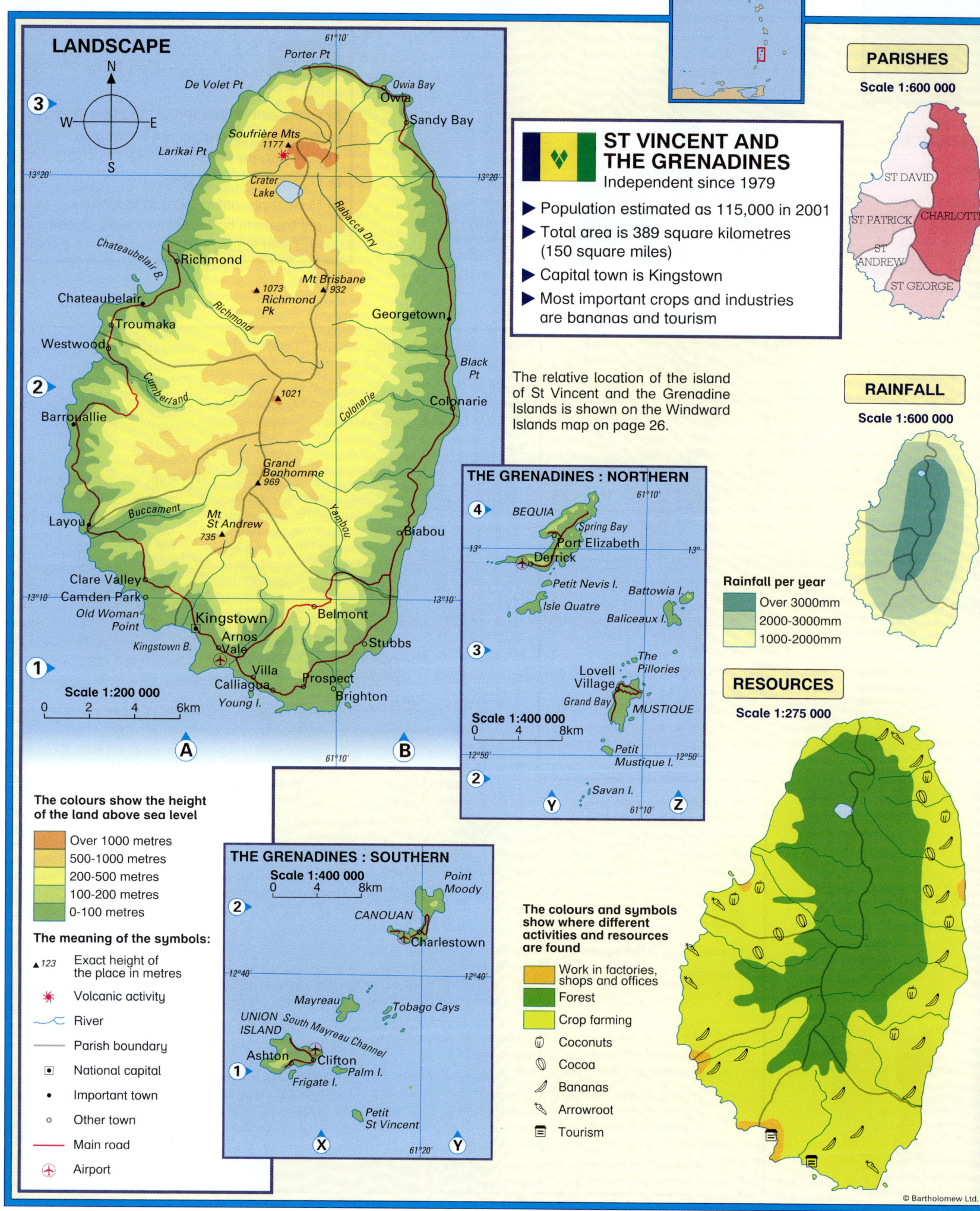

Grenada

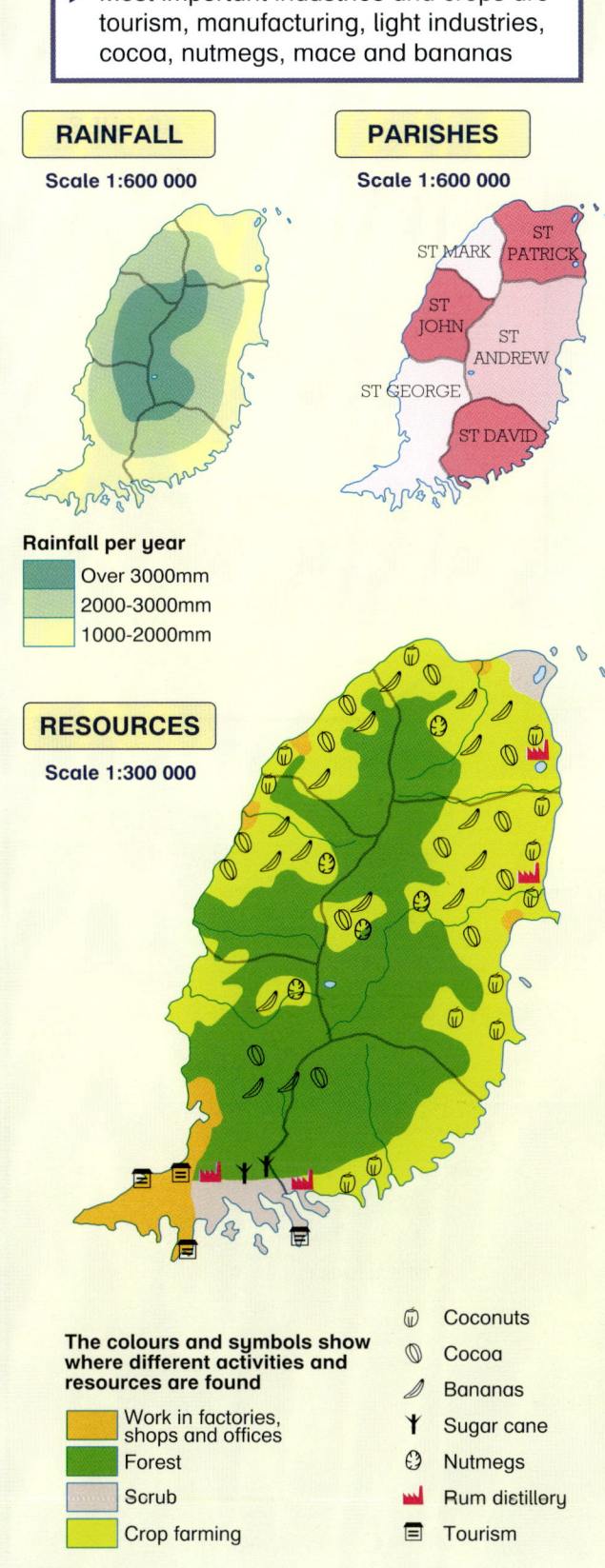

GRENADA
Independent since 1974

- Population estimated as 95,000 in 2001
- Total area is 345 square kilometres (133 square miles)
- Capital town is St George's
- Most important industries and crops are tourism, manufacturing, light industries, cocoa, nutmegs, mace and bananas

RAINFALL
Scale 1:600 000

Rainfall per year
- Over 3000mm
- 2000-3000mm
- 1000-2000mm

PARISHES
Scale 1:600 000

- ST MARK
- ST PATRICK
- ST JOHN
- ST ANDREW
- ST GEORGE
- ST DAVID

RESOURCES
Scale 1:300 000

The colours and symbols show where different activities and resources are found
- Work in factories, shops and offices
- Forest
- Scrub
- Crop farming

Symbols:
- Coconuts
- Cocoa
- Bananas
- Sugar cane
- Nutmegs
- Rum distillery
- Tourism

LANDSCAPE

The relative location of Grenada and its Grenadine islands, Carriacou and Petite Martinique, is shown on the Windward Islands map on page 26.

CARRIACOU & PETITE MARTINIQUE
Scale 1:200 000

Locations: Gun Point, North Point, Windward, Carriacou, Hillsborough Bay, Mabouya I., Hillsborough, Tarltons Point, Top Hill 235, Grand Bay, Tyrrel Bay, Hermitage, Kendeace Point, Manchineel Bay, White I., Saline I., Southwest Point, Frigate I., Large I., PETITE MARTINIQUE, GRENADA GRENADINES

Scale 1:200 000

Locations on main island: Sauters Bay, Sauteurs, Sugar Loaf I., Levera Pond, Green Island, Duquesne, Chantimelle, Victoria, R. Sallee, Lake Antoine, Tivoli, Gouyave, Mt St Catherine 840, La Poterie, Moya, Grand Roy, Simon, Great River, Telescope Pt, Concord, Birch Grove, Harford, Grenville, Grenville Bay, Marquis, Marquis I., Molinière Pt, Beausejour, Grand Etang, St Francis, Gt Bacolet Pt, Fontenoy, Mt Sinai 702, Pomme Rose, Crochu, St George's, Piedmontemps, St David's, Belmont, St Paul's, Grand Anse Bay, Grand Anse, Pt Salines, Frequente, Westerhall Point, Lance aux Epines, Pt of Fort Jeudy, Prickly Pt

The colours show the height of the land above sea level
- Over 500 metres
- 200-500 metres
- 100-200 metres
- 0-100 metres

The meaning of the symbols:
- ▲123 Exact height of the place in metres
- River
- Parish boundary
- National capital
- Important town
- Other town
- Main road
- Airport

© Bartholomew Ltd.

29

Barbados

LANDSCAPE

The colours show the height of the land above sea level
- 200-500 metres
- 100-200 metres
- 0-100 metres

The meaning of the symbols:
- ▲123 Exact height of the place in metres
- Water course
- Parish boundary
- ⊡ National capital
- • Important town
- ○ Village
- Highway
- Main road
- ✈ Airport

BARBADOS
Independent since 1966

- Population estimated as 260,000 in 2001
- Total area is 430 square kilometres (166 square miles)
- Capital town is Bridgetown
- Most important industries are tourism, sugar cultivation and processing, light industries, fishing and financial services

PARISHES
Scale 1:400 000

- ST LUCY
- ST PETER
- ST ANDREW
- ST JAMES
- ST JOSEPH
- ST THOMAS
- ST JOHN
- ST GEORGE
- ST MICHAEL
- ST PHILIP
- CHRISTCHURCH

Places and features

North Point, Archers Bay, The Spout, Greenidge, Archers, Spring Hall, Cockold Pt, Paul's Pt, Harrison Point, Checker Hall, Boscobelle, Fustic, Mt. Stepney 245, Six Men's Bay, Mile and a Quarter, 147, Greenland, Speightstown, Long Pond, Belleplaine, 169, 277, Upper Carlton, Westmoreland, Mt. Hillaby 340, Cattlewash, Lower Carlton, Hillaby, Bruce Vale, Joe's River, Bathsheba, Hillcrest, Alleynes Bay, Orange Hill, Mt. Misery 326, Chimborazo, Castle Grant 338, 306, Congor Rocks, Holetown, Rock Hall, Welchman Hall, Coffee Gully, Clifton Hall, Glebe, Conset Bay, Conset Pt, Arch Hall, St Marks, Bell Pt, Paynes Bay, Four Cross Roads, Massiah Street, Marley Vale, Ragged Pt, Bridgefield, Redman's Village, 228, Belair, Workmans, 164, Kitridge Pt, Fitts Village, Jackson, Rowans, Church Village, Wellhouse, 123, Warrens, Hothersal Turning, Robinsons, Black Rock, Marchfield, Six Cross Roads, Brighton, Bush Hall, Brereton, Four Roads, The Crane, Howells, Mapp Hill, Boarded Hall, Cobbler's Rock, Foul Bay, Mount Friendship, St Patricks, 62, Bridgetown, 83, Sargeants Village, St Martins, Carlisle Bay, Garrison, Vauxhall, Salt Cave Pt, Needham's Point, Hastings, Worthing, Lodge Road, Welches, Providence, Chancery Lane, Oistins, Thornbury Hill, Long Bay, Oistins Bay, Enterprise, Silver Sands, South Pt

Scale 1:145 000
0 1 2 3 4 5km

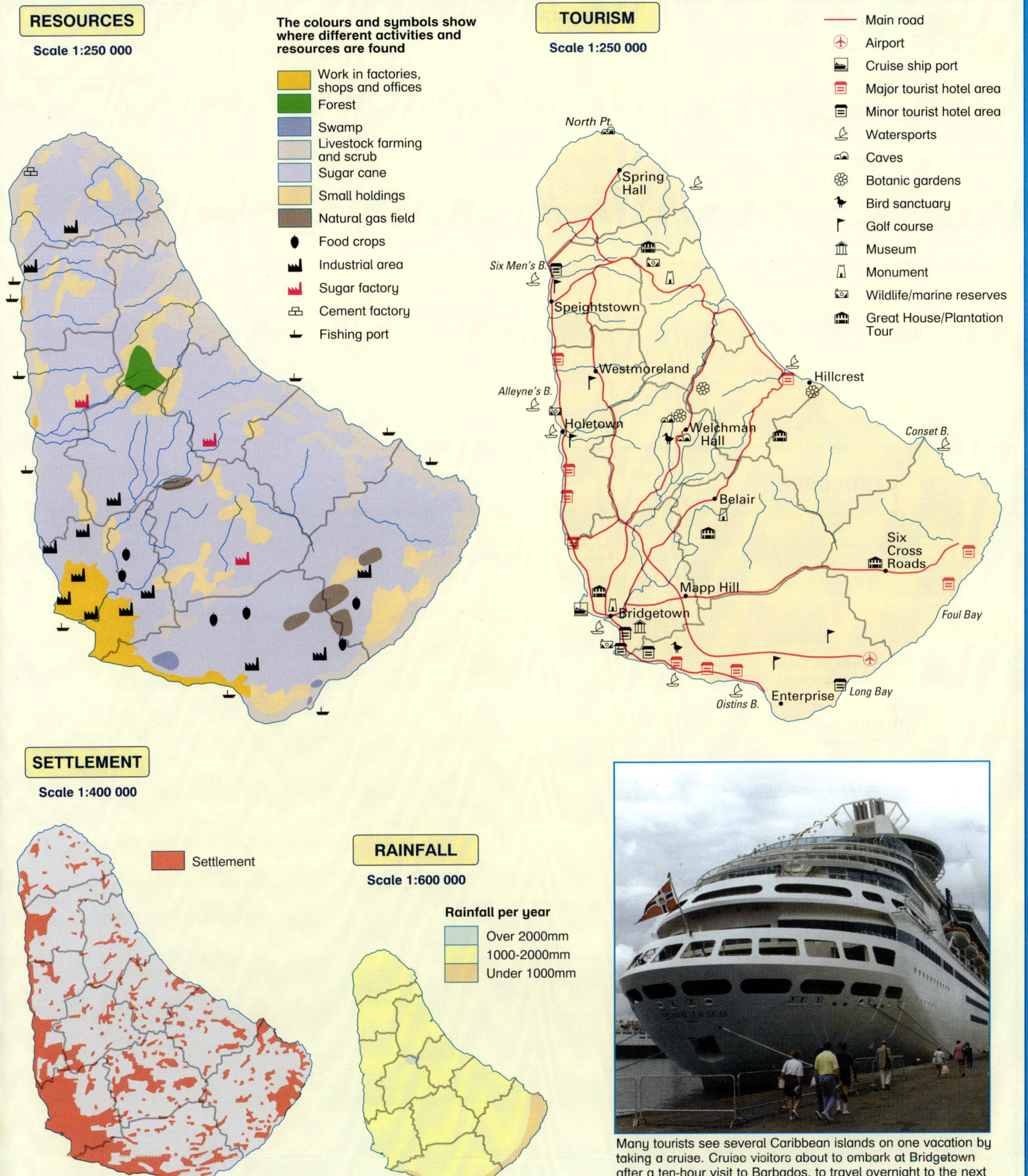

Trinidad and Tobago

TRINIDAD AND TOBAGO
Independent since 1962

- Population estimated as 1,330,000 in 2001
- Total area is 5,128 square kilometres (1,980 square miles)
- Capital city is Port-of-Spain
  Chief town of Tobago is Scarborough
- Most important industries are petroleum, petroleum products, chemicals, sugar and tourism

LOCAL GOVERNMENT
Scale 1:1 250 000

- DIEGO MARTIN
- SAN JUAN-LAVENTILLE
- PORT-OF-SPAIN
- TUNAPUNA-PIARCO
- ARIMA
- SANGRE GRANDE
- CHAGUANAS
- COUVA-TABAQUITE-TALPARO
- RIO CLARO-MAYARO
- SAN FERNANDO
- POINT FORTIN
- PRINCES TOWN
- PENAL-DEBE
- SIPARIA

Legend:
- City
- Borough
- Regional Corporation

COUNTIES
Scale 1:2 500 000

- ST GEORGE
- ST DAVID
- ST ANDREW
- CARONI
- NARIVA
- VICTORIA
- MAYARO
- ST PATRICK

LANDSCAPE

The colours show the height of the land above sea level
- Over 500 metres
- 200-500 metres
- 100-200 metres
- 0-100 metres

The meaning of the symbols:
- ▲123 Exact height of the place in metres
- River
- International boundary
- County boundary
- National capital
- Important town
- Other town
- Main road
- International airport

Scale 1:600 000

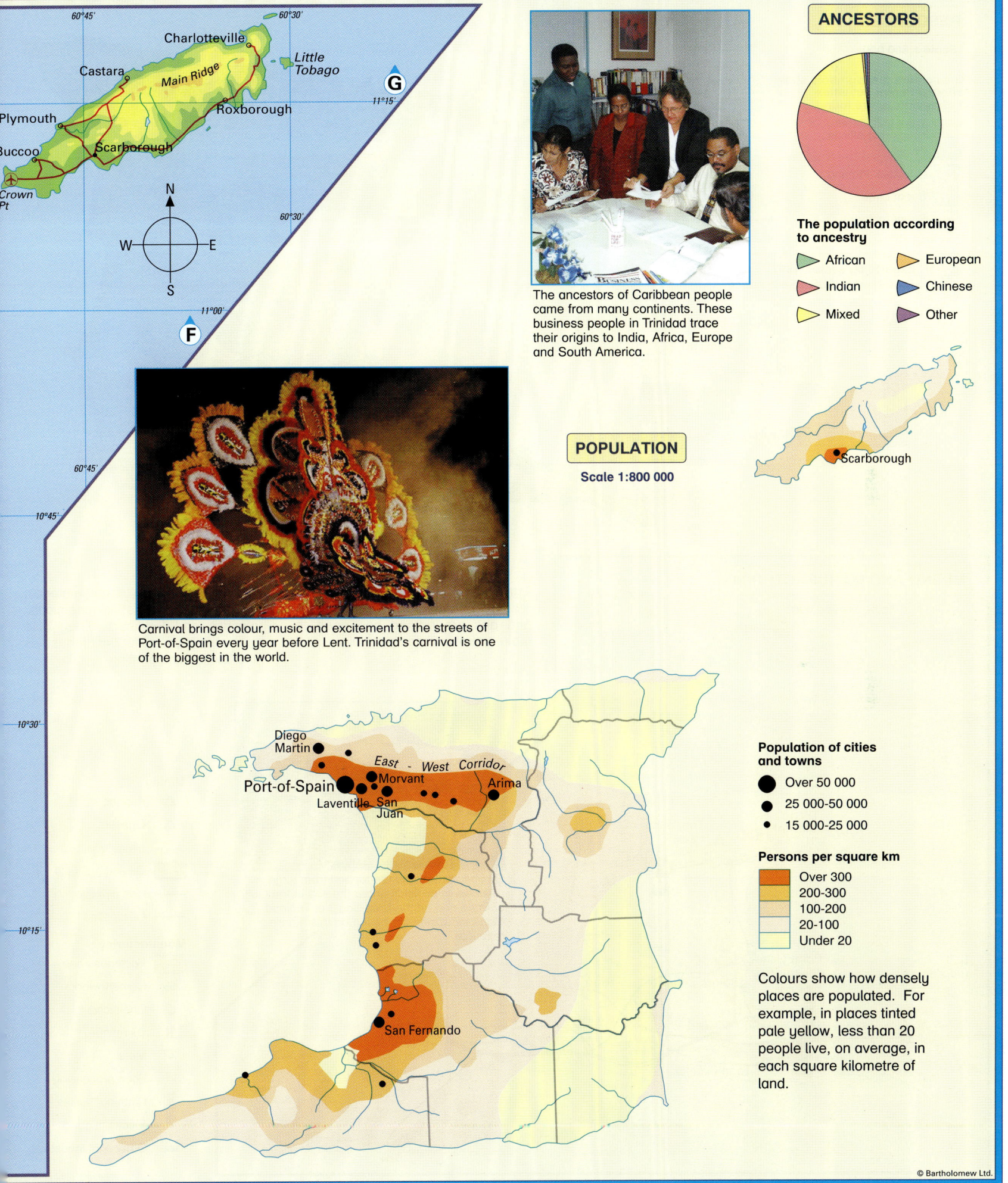

34 Trinidad : Resources

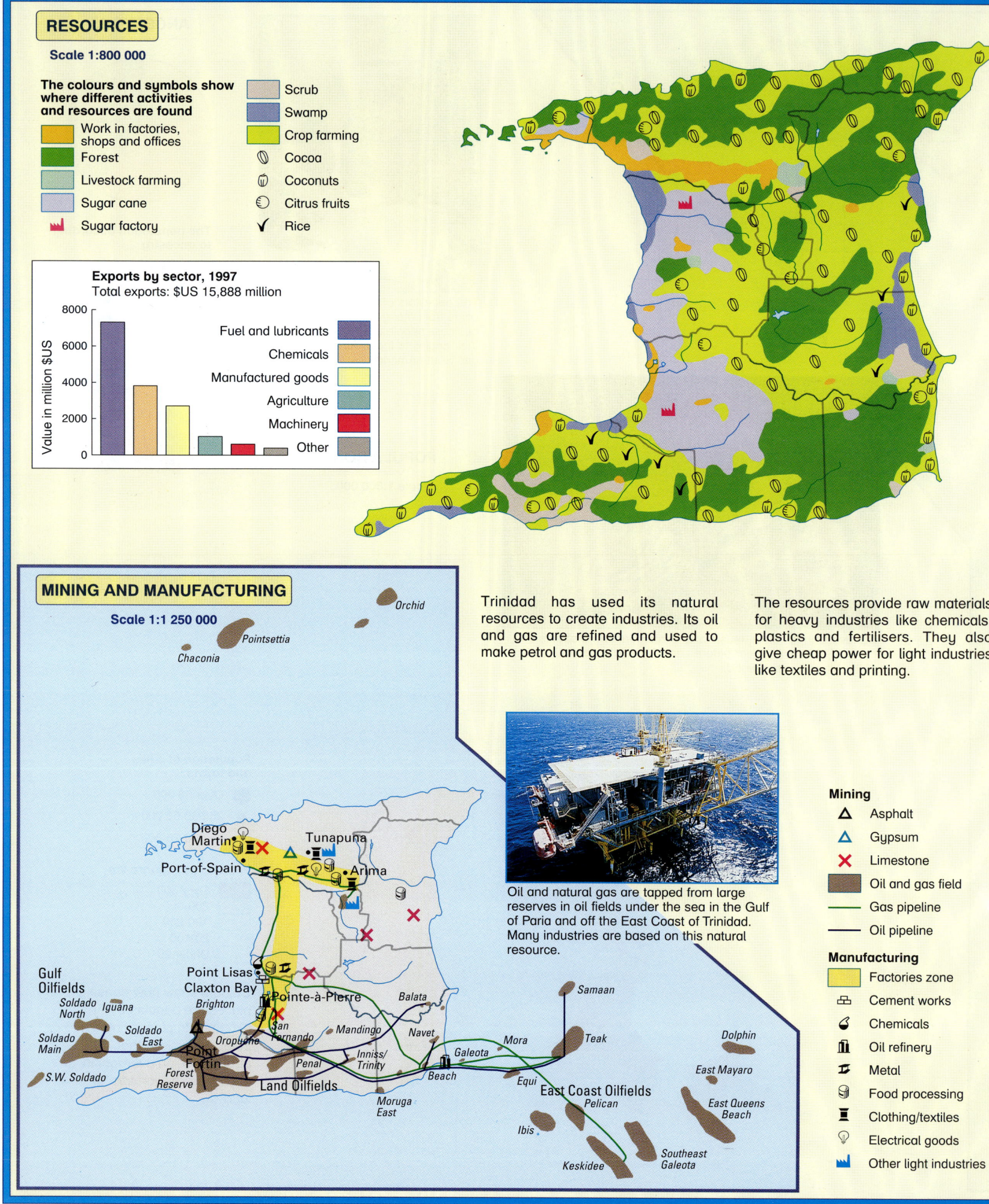

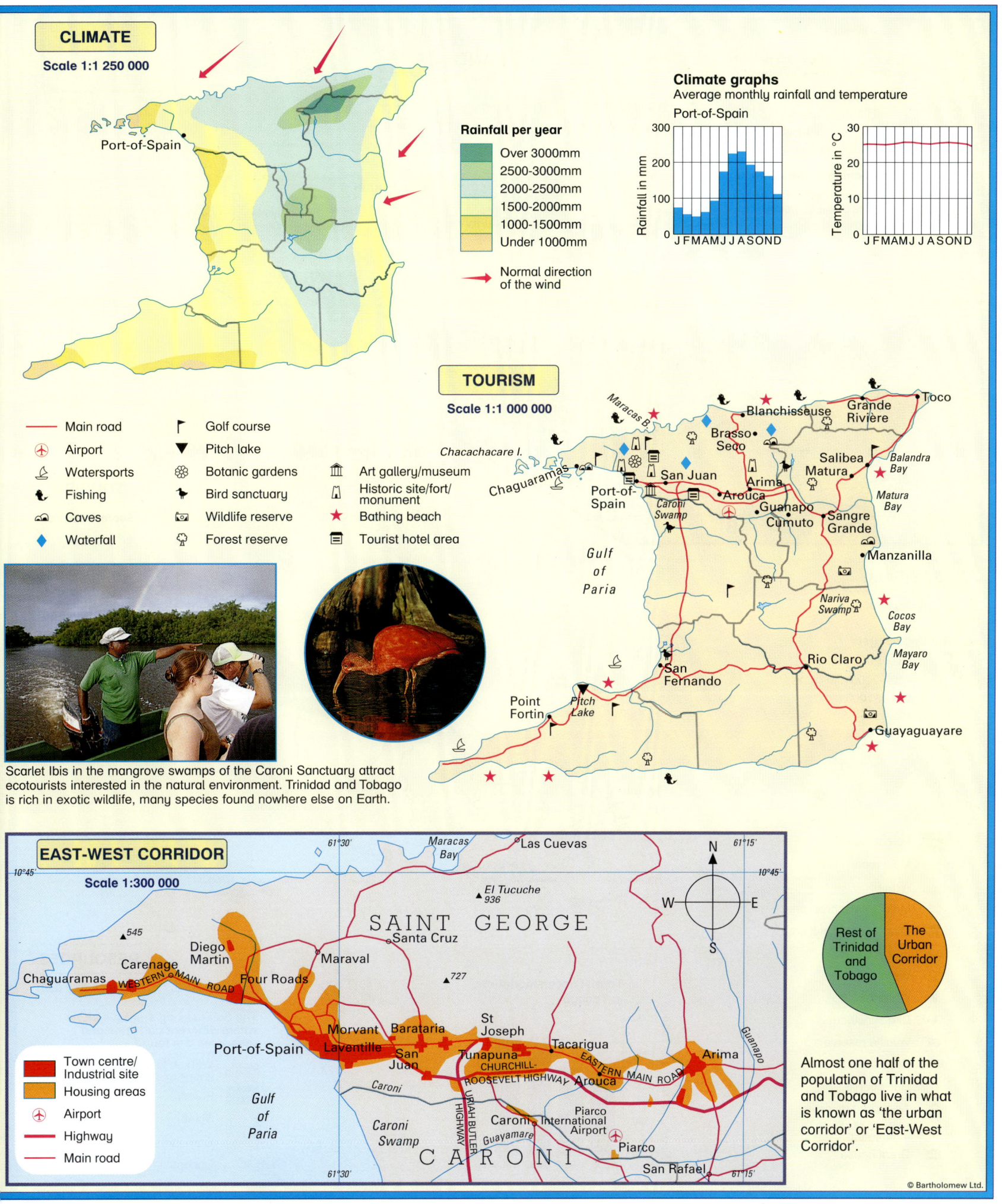

Tobago

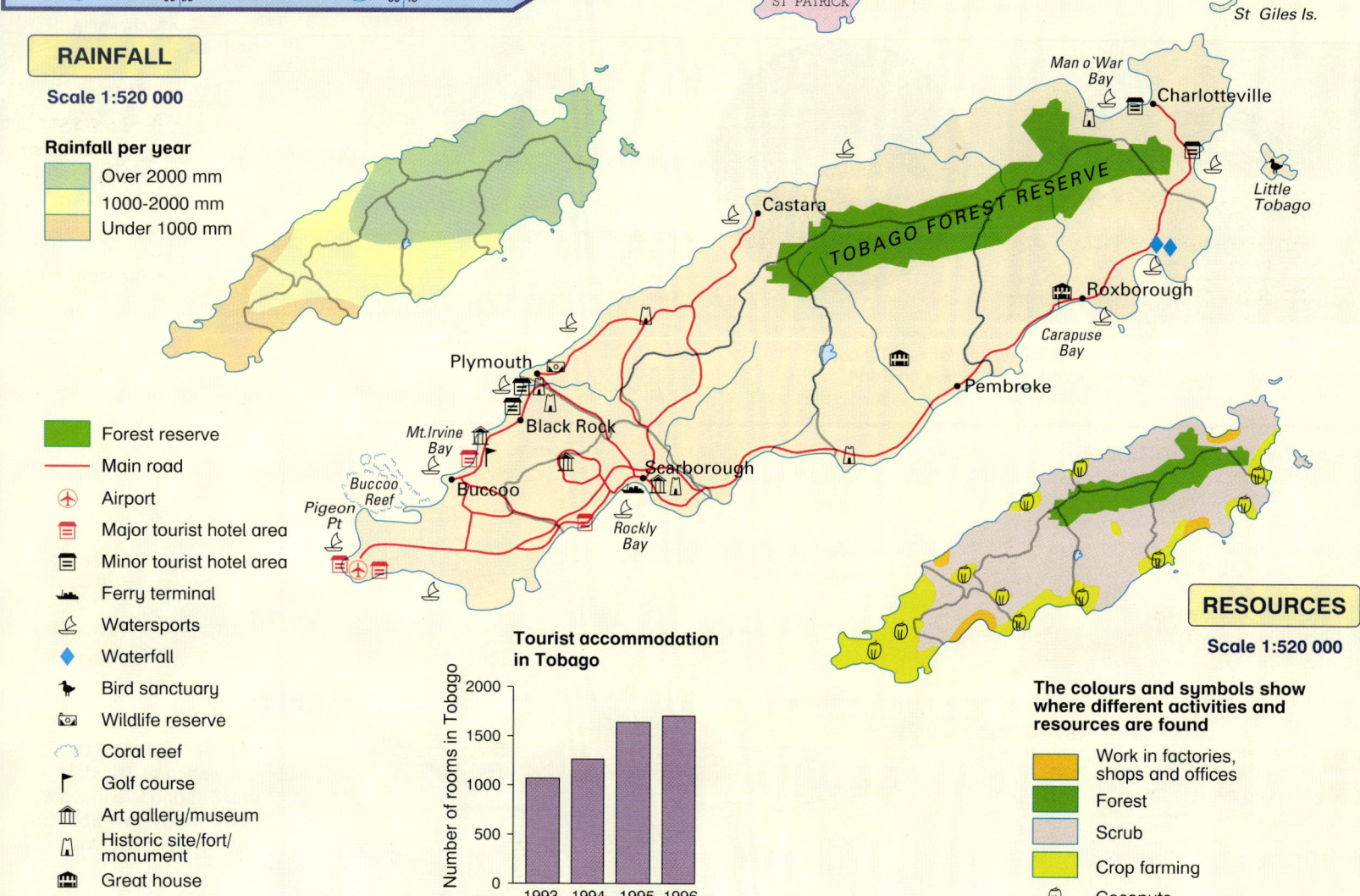

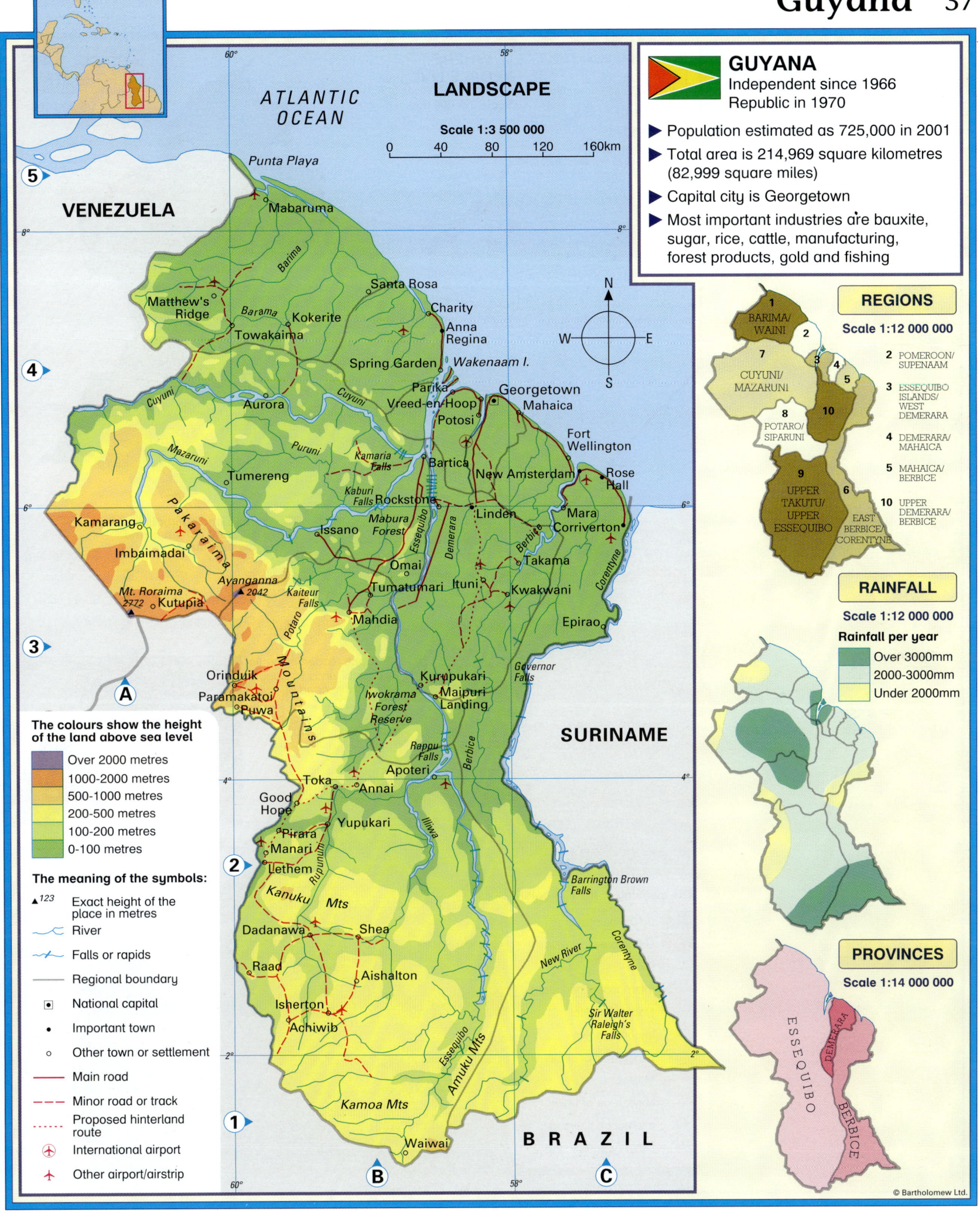

Guyana

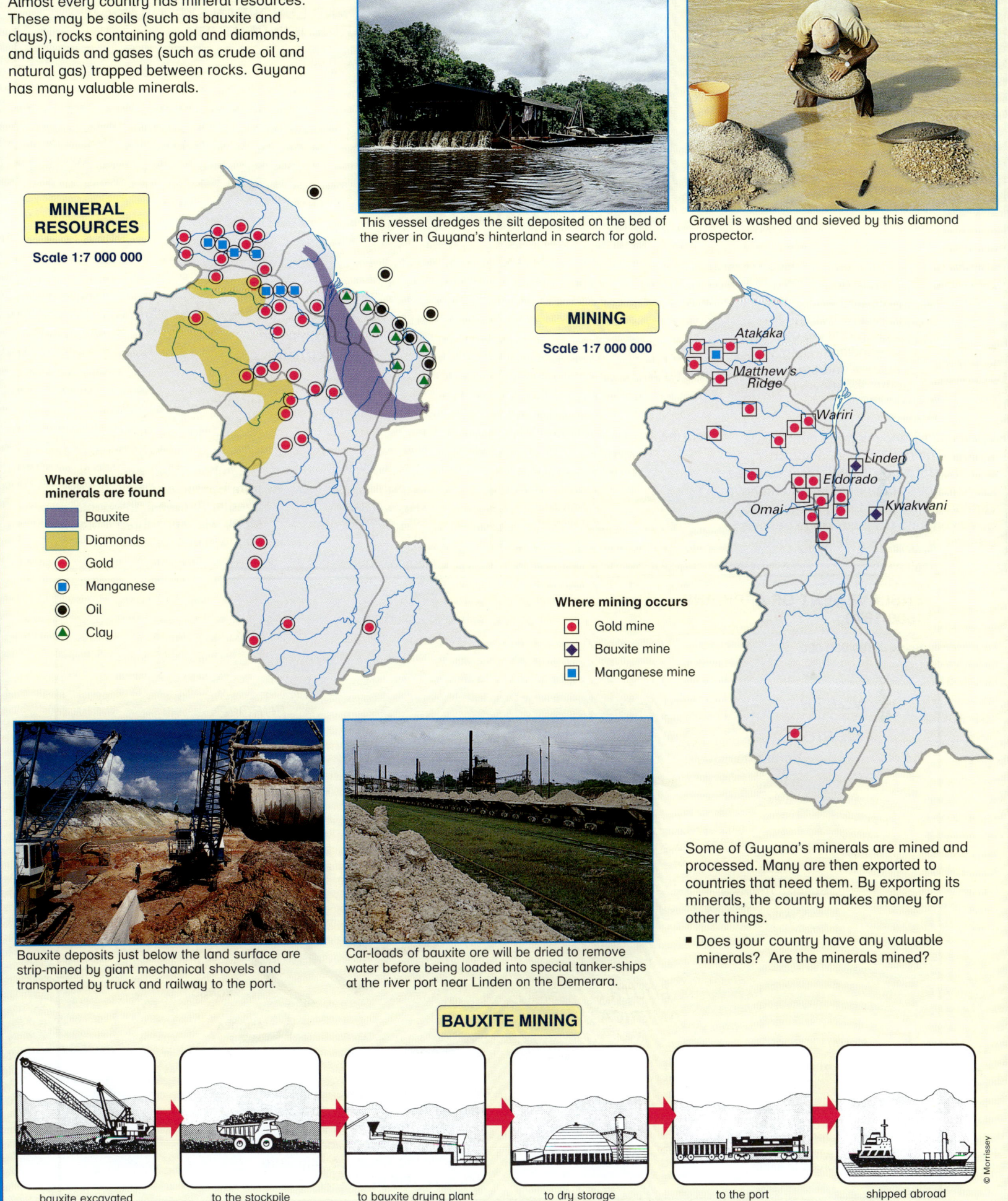

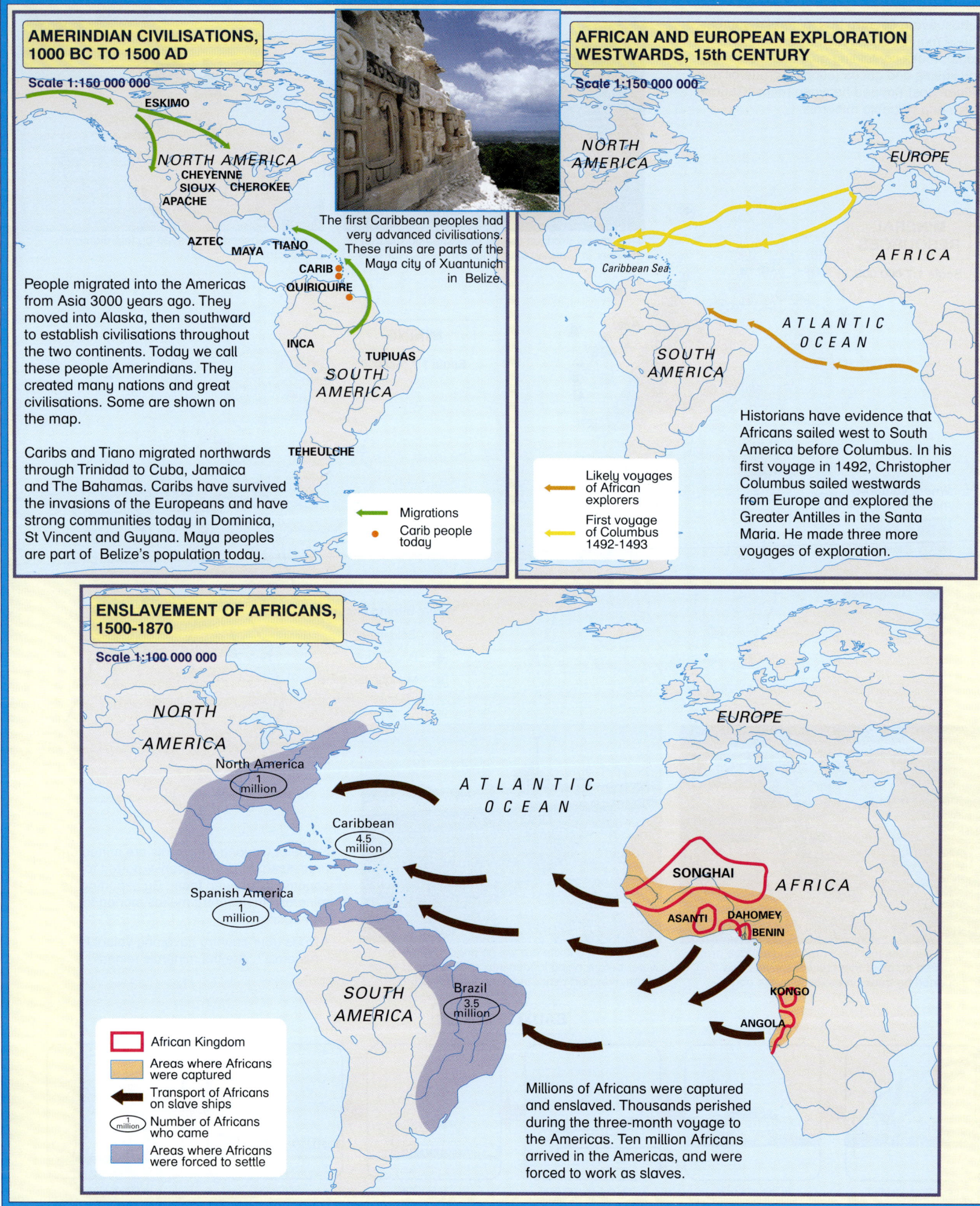

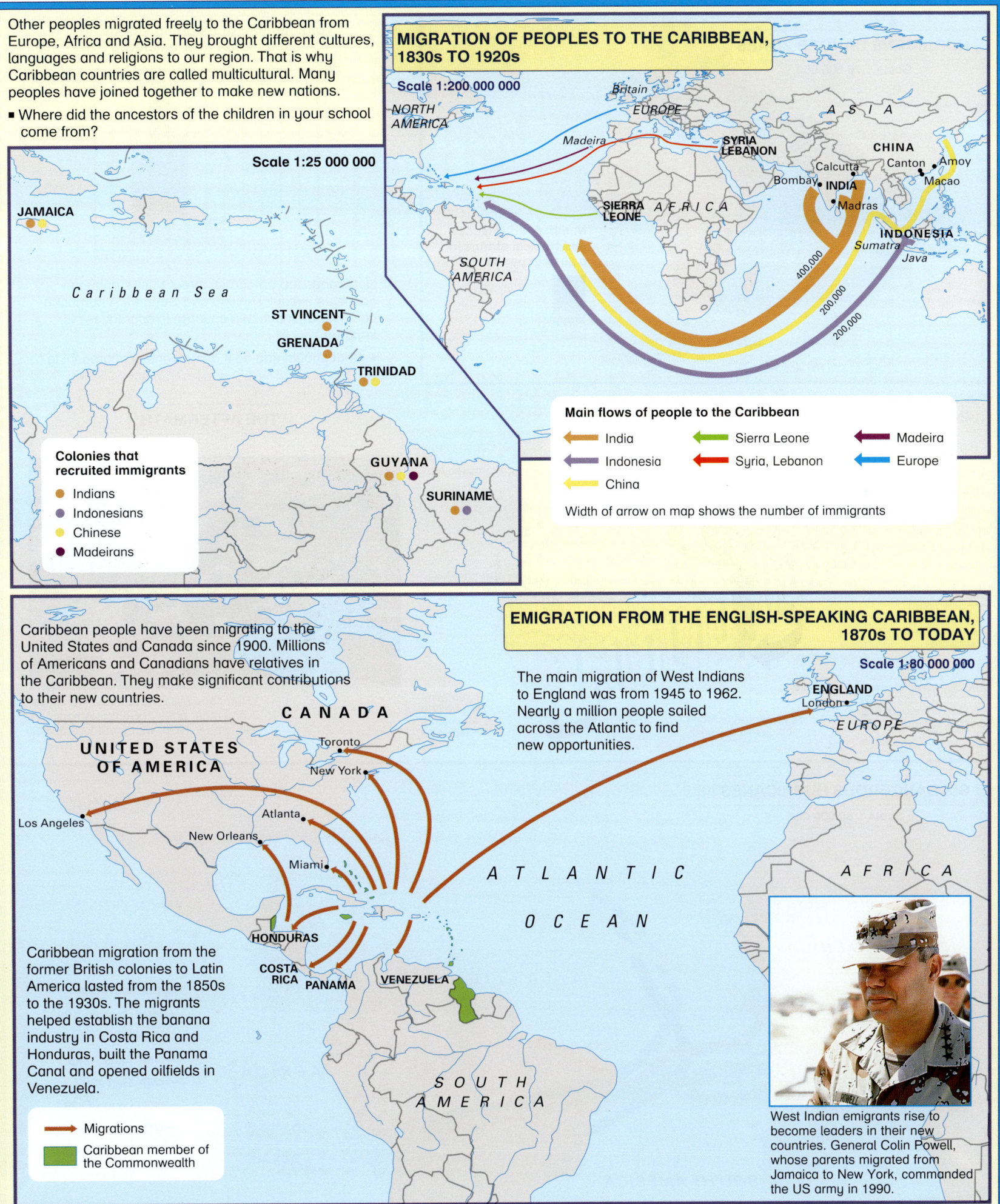

Other peoples migrated freely to the Caribbean from Europe, Africa and Asia. They brought different cultures, languages and religions to our region. That is why Caribbean countries are called multicultural. Many peoples have joined together to make new nations.

- Where did the ancestors of the children in your school come from?

MIGRATION OF PEOPLES TO THE CARIBBEAN, 1830s TO 1920s

Scale 1:200 000 000

Main flows of people to the Caribbean
- India
- Indonesia
- China
- Sierra Leone
- Syria, Lebanon
- Madeira
- Europe

Width of arrow on map shows the number of immigrants

Scale 1:25 000 000

Colonies that recruited immigrants
- Indians
- Indonesians
- Chinese
- Madeirans

EMIGRATION FROM THE ENGLISH-SPEAKING CARIBBEAN, 1870s TO TODAY

Scale 1:80 000 000

Caribbean people have been migrating to the United States and Canada since 1900. Millions of Americans and Canadians have relatives in the Caribbean. They make significant contributions to their new countries.

The main migration of West Indians to England was from 1945 to 1962. Nearly a million people sailed across the Atlantic to find new opportunities.

Caribbean migration from the former British colonies to Latin America lasted from the 1850s to the 1930s. The migrants helped establish the banana industry in Costa Rica and Honduras, built the Panama Canal and opened oilfields in Venezuela.

- Migrations
- Caribbean member of the Commonwealth

West Indian emigrants rise to become leaders in their new countries. General Colin Powell, whose parents migrated from Jamaica to New York, commanded the US army in 1990.

© Bartholomew Ltd.

42 Hurricanes

HURRICANE DANGER ZONES
Scale 1:70 000 000

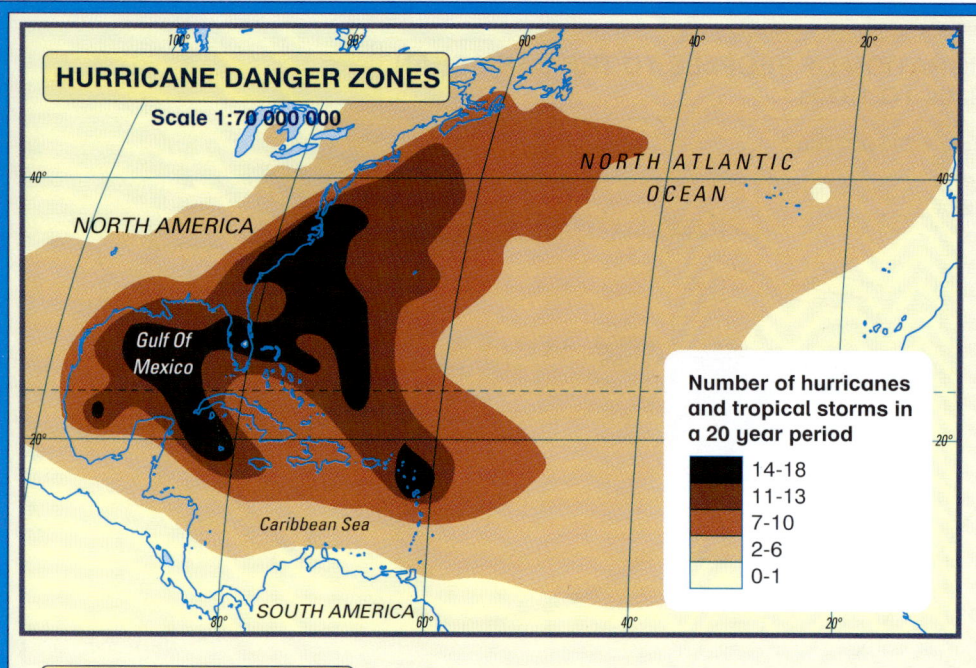

Number of hurricanes and tropical storms in a 20 year period
- 14-18
- 11-13
- 7-10
- 2-6
- 0-1

Total number of recorded storms for each month over a century

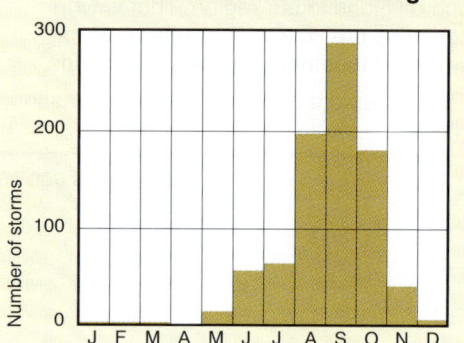

Hurricanes are an annual threat to all Caribbean countries except Trinidad and Guyana. A hurricane can destroy much of a country. Preparedness is important.

■ What should you do if a hurricane is approaching?

INSIDE A HURRICANE

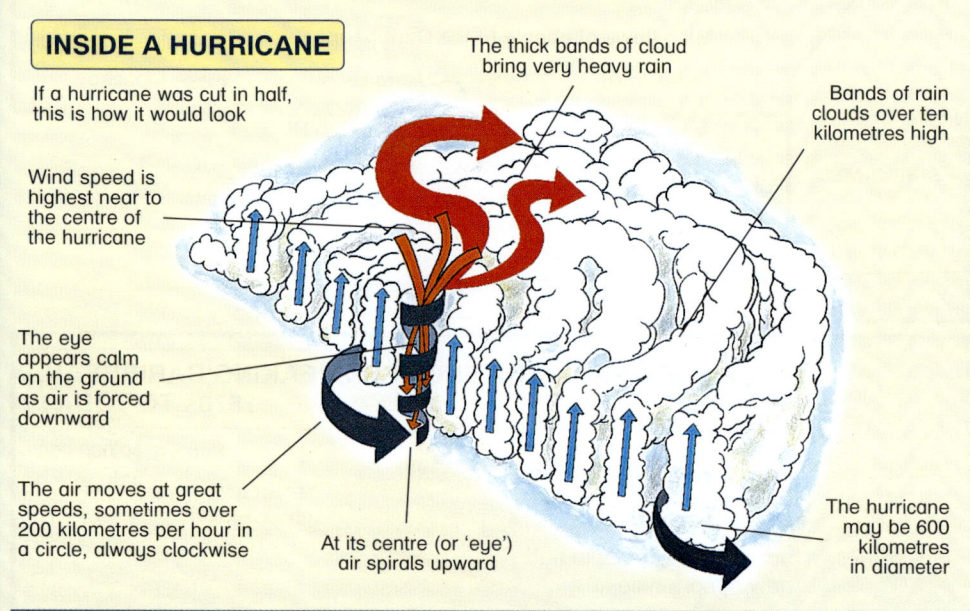

- If a hurricane was cut in half, this is how it would look
- Wind speed is highest near to the centre of the hurricane
- The eye appears calm on the ground as air is forced downward
- The air moves at great speeds, sometimes over 200 kilometres per hour in a circle, always clockwise
- At its centre (or 'eye') air spirals upward
- The thick bands of cloud bring very heavy rain
- Bands of rain clouds over ten kilometres high
- The hurricane may be 600 kilometres in diameter

THE AFTERMATH

Hurricane Mitch devastated Honduras and other parts of Central America in November 1998, with great loss of life.

SIX DANGEROUS HURRICANES
Scale 1:80 000 000

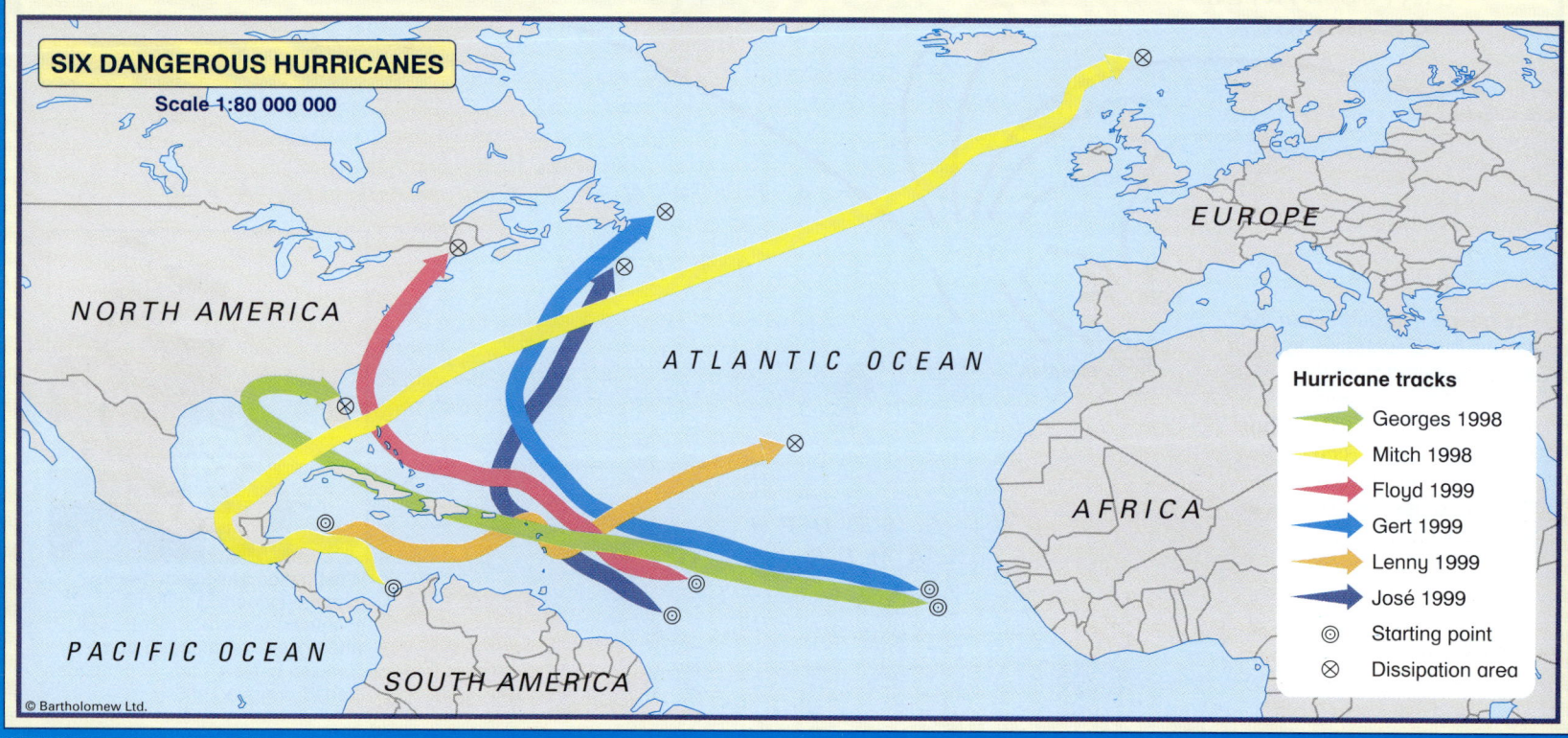

Hurricane tracks
- Georges 1998
- Mitch 1998
- Floyd 1999
- Gert 1999
- Lenny 1999
- José 1999
- ◎ Starting point
- ⊗ Dissipation area

© Bartholomew Ltd.

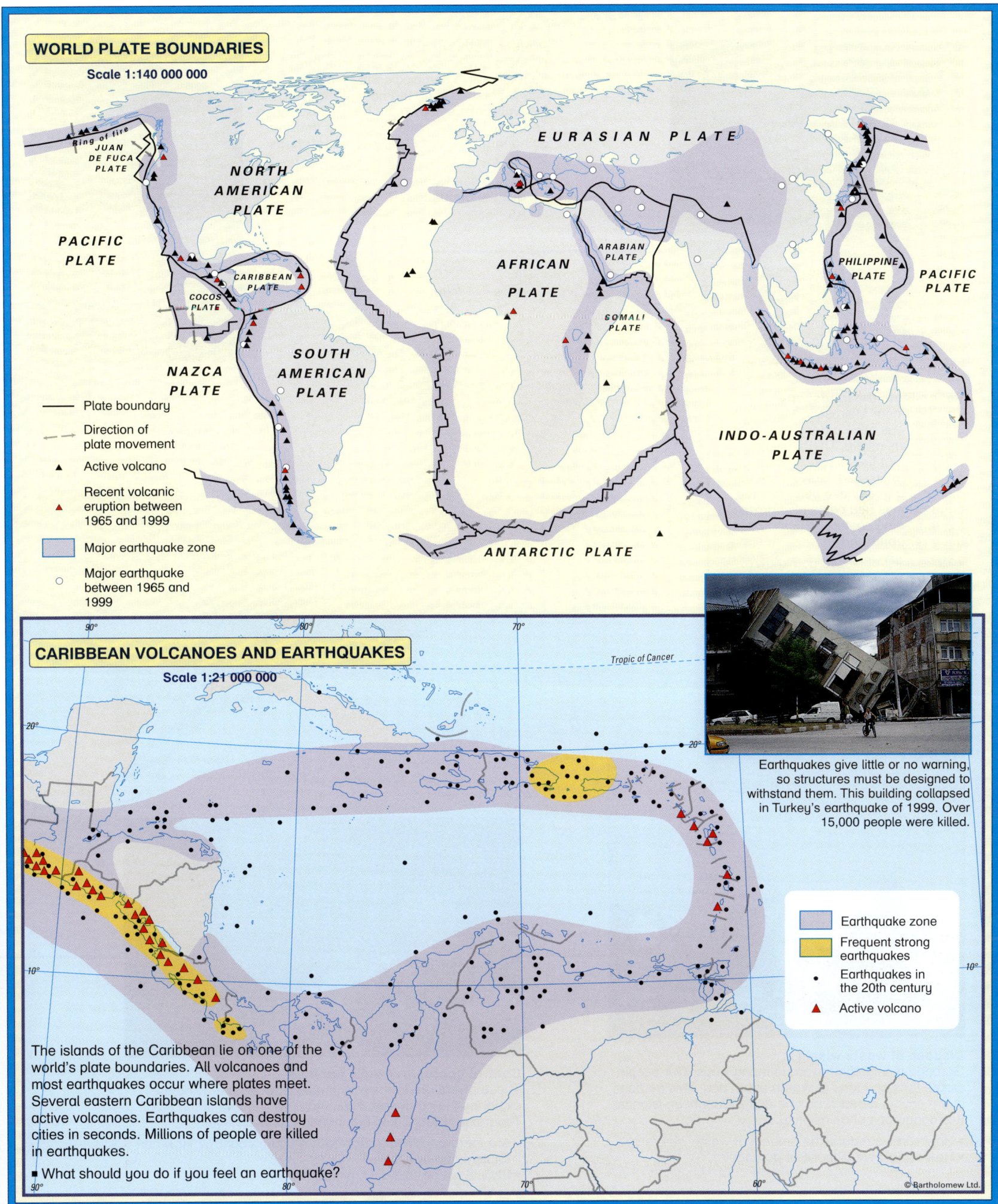

44 Caribbean : Conserving our Resources

Protect watersheds
Farmers have cleared much of the forest from this hill in Jamaica's Blue Mountains. The watershed is on the ridge. When it rains, the water rushes down the hill. Soil is eroded. The farmers lose their crops. Their families go hungry. It is better to leave **watersheds** forested.

- Can you see where rain water has caused a gully to be formed?

Rehabilitate the landscape
This land near Melrose in Manchester, Jamaica was once a deep pit where bauxite was mined. The bauxite company put the soil back when mining was finished. Now Honduras mahogany trees have been planted on the slopes and cattle also graze the remaining pasture. The land has been **rehabilitated**.

- Make a list of places you know that have been left in ruins by human activity.
- How could these places be made useful and beautiful again?

Dispose of waste wisely
Garbage is a health hazard in many ways. Our people create tons and tons of **waste** every day. This garbage dump covers a beach on one of the Caribbean islands. It is dangerous and unsightly.

- How can we reduce the amount of waste we create?
- How should we dispose of garbage?

Control access to fragile habitats
These divers are tourists off the coast of Belize. They are exploring the coral reef. They may break some of the coral. Too many divers could damage the reefs for ever.

- Are there any **fragile habitats** on your country? How can tourism damage them?
- Should we protect such places?

Maintain air quality
This methanol factory in Trinidad used to discharge dust, fumes and chemicals into the air. Workers and people nearby got lung diseases. Now the problem has been solved by controls and filters, and the air around the factory is clean. The **quality of the air** has improved. People must insist that factories do not discharge poisons into the air, rivers or the sea.

- Can you think of any factories which pollute the environment?

Protect endangered species from extinction
This whale was in the Caribbean Sea, off the coast of Dominica. Whales are an **endangered species**. Japanese and Norwegian ships capture and kill whales for their meat and oil. If whaling does not stop, whales will become an extinct species.

- Do you think whales should be protected?

Regulate shipping in the Caribbean Sea
Some countries send their ships full of dangerous radioactive waste through the Caribbean Sea. If a ship carrying plutonium or other dangerous waste material had an accident, the Caribbean would be **polluted** and the sea would be poisoned. These Greenpeace demonstrators were trying to stop the ship you can see passing through the Panama Canal because it was carrying nuclear waste.

- What can we do to protect the Caribbean Sea from such dangers?

Conserve our rainforest
This is some of the last tropical **rainforest** in the world. It is at the Kaieteur Falls in Guyana. Undiscovered plant and animal life is in the rainforest and these are a resource for the future. The trees must be protected, and replanted if they are harvested.

- Is there any virgin rainforest left in your country?

© Bartholomew Ltd.

48 World Political

Cities and towns
- Capital cities
- Important towns

THE COMMONWEALTH

There are 54 countries of the world, from all the continents, that have joined together as The Commonwealth of Nations. Most were, long ago, part of the British Empire. Nearly all of them use English as their official language. Thirteen of the CARICOM countries, and the five British Overseas Territories in the Caribbean, are members of the Commonwealth. Countries of the Commonwealth help each other in many ways, and compete in sports.

- Make a list of countries that are Commonwealth members.

A.	ALBANIA	C.	CROATIA
AR.	ARMENIA	CAM.	CAMEROON
AU.	AUSTRIA	C.A.R.	CENTRAL AFRICAN REPUBLIC
AZ.	AZERBAIJAN		
B.	BELGIUM	C.R.	CZECH REPUBLIC
BE.	BENIN	GER.	GERMANY
B.H.	BOSNIA-HERZEGOVINA	H.	HUNGARY

© Bartholomew Ltd.

L.	LUXEMBOURG	SW.	SWITZERLAND
Li.	LITHUANIA	T.	TOGO
M.	MACEDONIA	TA.	TAJIKISTAN
MO.	MOLDOVA	TURK.	TURKMENISTAN
N.	NETHERLANDS	U.A.E.	UNITED ARAB EMIRATES
S.	SLOVENIA	Y.	YUGOSLAVIA
SL.	SLOVAKIA		

THE UNITED NATIONS

Representatives of the governments of all the countries of the world meet together in one organisation called the United Nations. They work together to try to prevent war, disease, poverty, and environmental destruction. They also work to improve the level of health and education all over the world, and establish rights for women, children and minority peoples who are sometimes treated badly. There are many United Nations organisations for special purposes and their names all begin with UN.

■ Name three UN organisations and say what they do.

50 North America Relief

North America Countries 51

52 South America Relief

South America Countries 53

54 Europe Relief

Europe Countries 55

56 Asia Relief

Africa Relief

Africa Countries

60 Oceania Relief

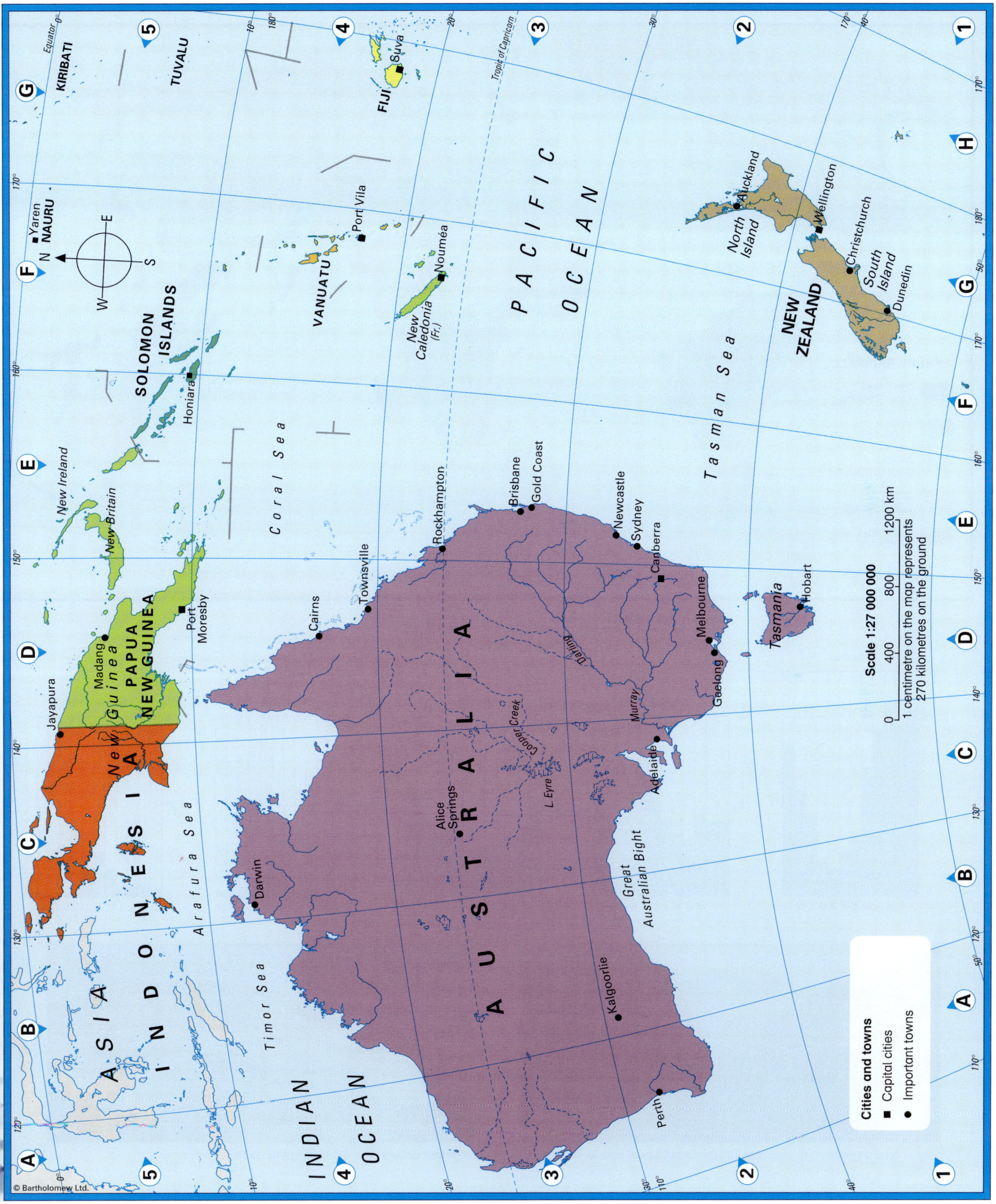
AUSTRALIA
PAPUA NEW GUINEA
INDONESIA
ASIA
NEW ZEALAND
SOLOMON ISLANDS
VANUATU
FIJI
NAURU
KIRIBATI
TUVALU
PACIFIC OCEAN
INDIAN OCEAN
Tasman Sea
Coral Sea
Arafura Sea
Timor Sea
Great Australian Bight
New Guinea
New Britain
New Ireland
New Caledonia (Fr.)
North Island
South Island
Tasmania
L. Eyre
Cooper Creek
Darling
Murray
Perth
Kalgoorlie
Darwin
Alice Springs
Adelaide
Geelong
Melbourne
Canberra
Sydney
Newcastle
Gold Coast
Brisbane
Rockhampton
Townsville
Cairns
Hobart
Port Moresby
Madang
Jayapura
Honiara
Port Vila
Nouméa
Suva
Yaren
Auckland
Wellington
Christchurch
Dunedin
Equator
Tropic of Capricorn
Scale 1:27 000 000
0 400 800 1200 km
1 centimetre on the map represents 270 kilometres on the ground
Cities and towns
Capital cities
Important towns
© Bartholomew Ltd.

62 World Climate

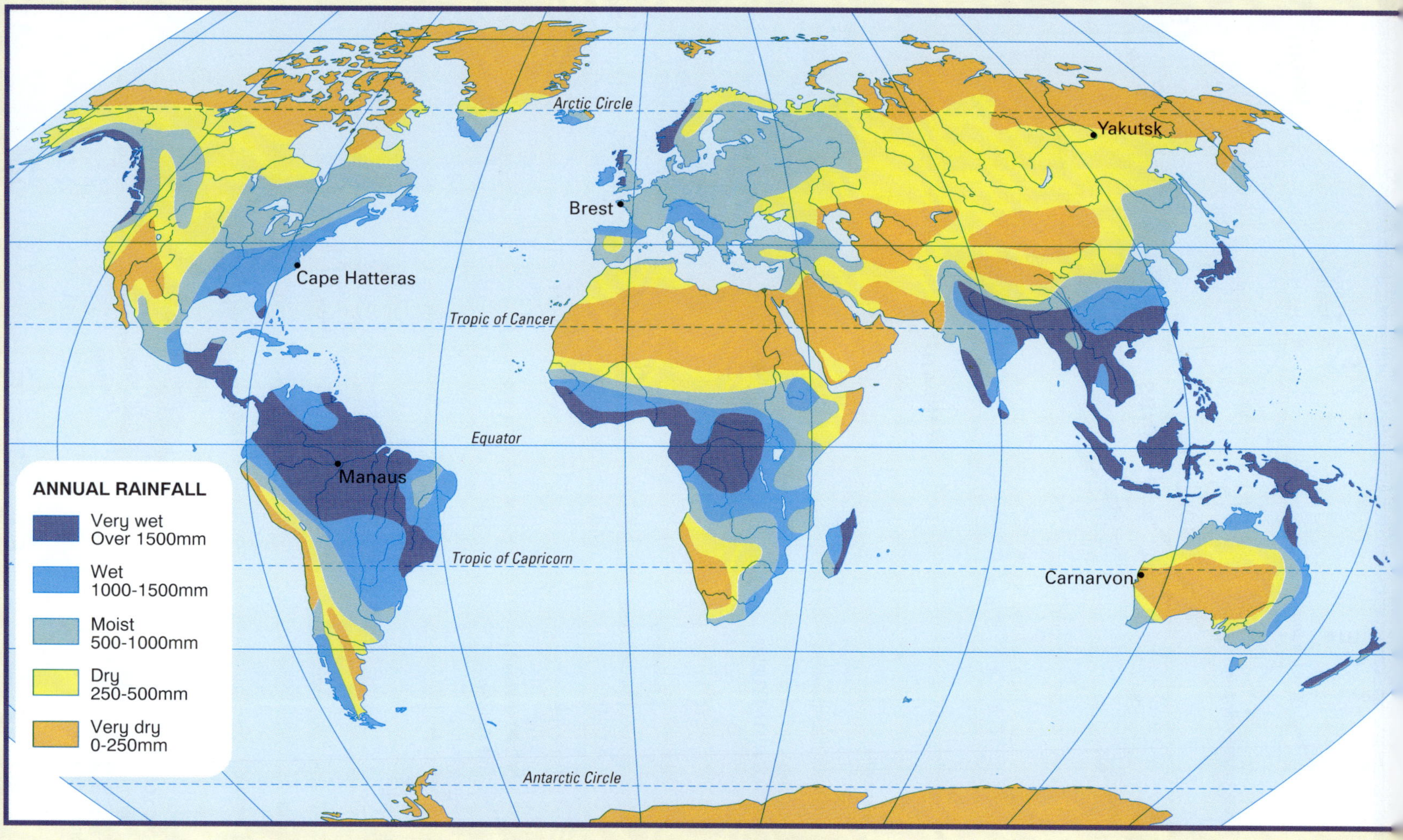

ANNUAL RAINFALL

- Very wet — Over 1500mm
- Wet — 1000-1500mm
- Moist — 500-1000mm
- Dry — 250-500mm
- Very dry — 0-250mm

CLIMATE GRAPHS
Average monthly rainfall

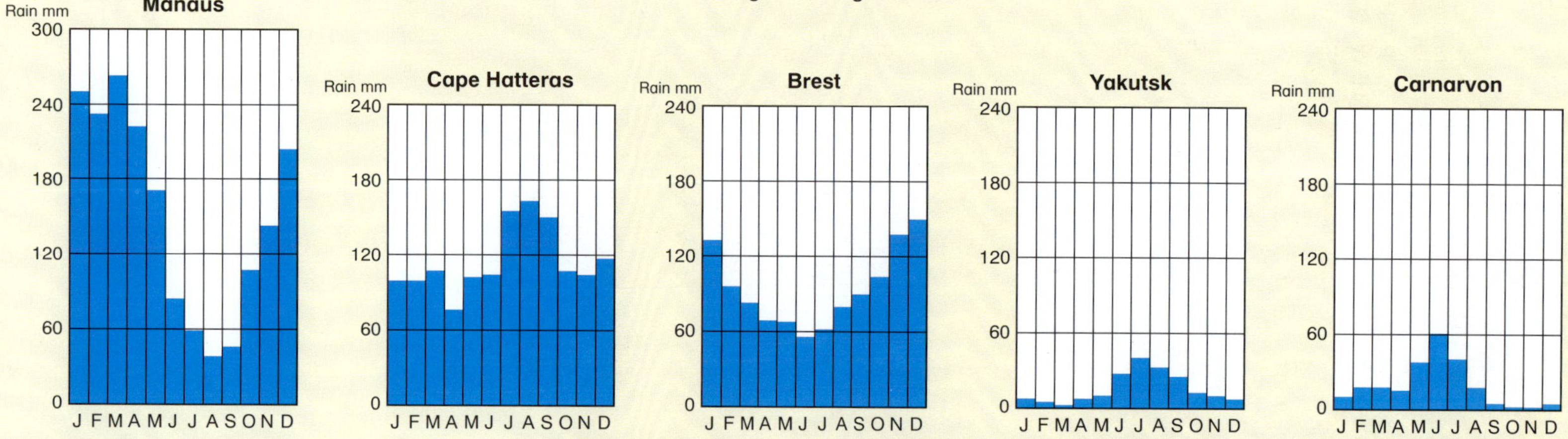

Manaus • Cape Hatteras • Brest • Yakutsk • Carnarvon

The natural vegetation of very wet, hot areas is tropical rain forest

A desert occurs where it is very dry and hot

© Bartholomew Ltd.

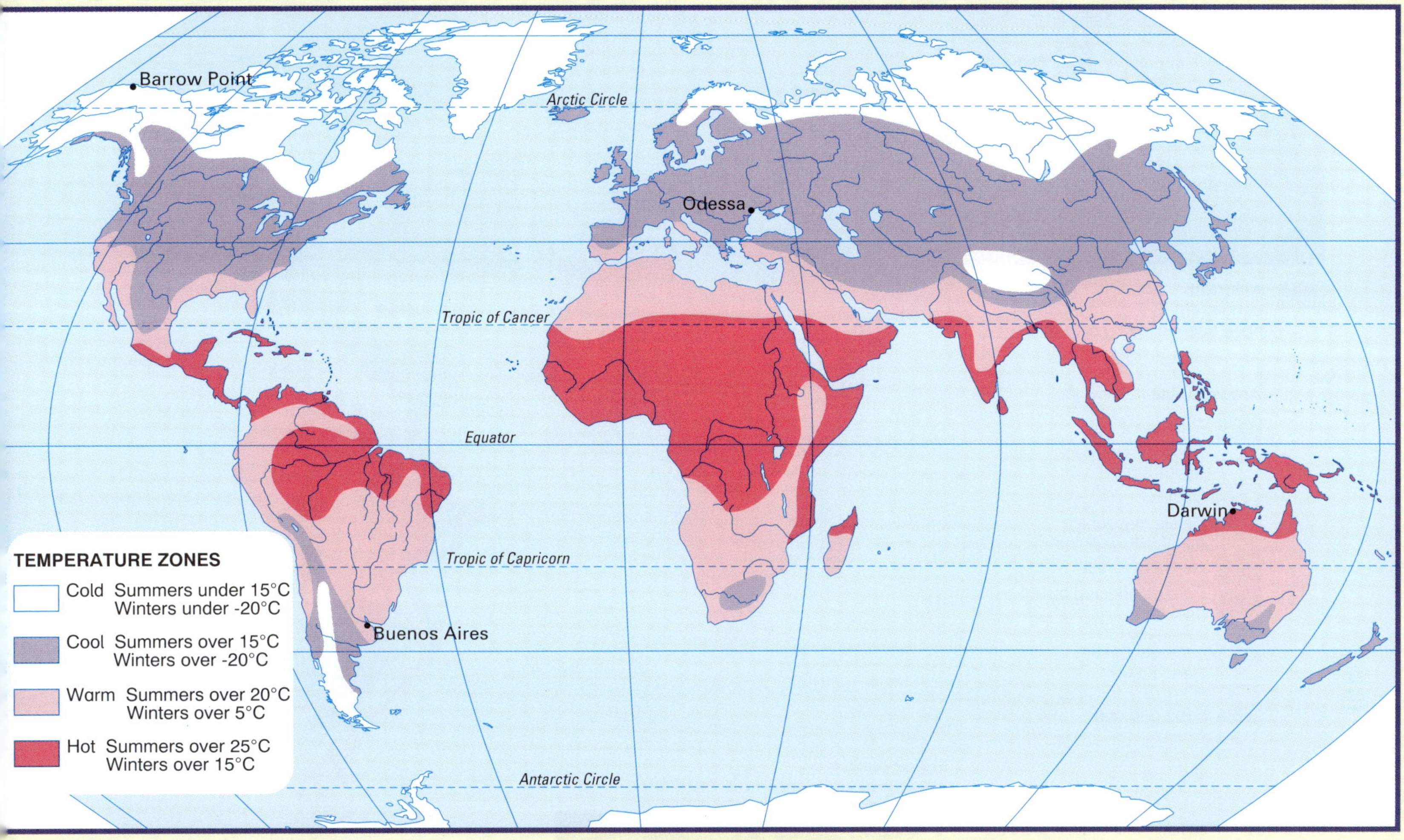

Barrow Point
Arctic Circle
Odessa
Tropic of Cancer
Equator
Darwin
Tropic of Capricorn
Buenos Aires
Antarctic Circle
TEMPERATURE ZONES
Cold Summers under 15°C Winters under -20°C
Cool Summers over 15°C Winters over -20°C
Warm Summers over 20°C Winters over 5°C
Hot Summers over 25°C Winters over 15°C

CLIMATE GRAPHS

Average monthly temperature

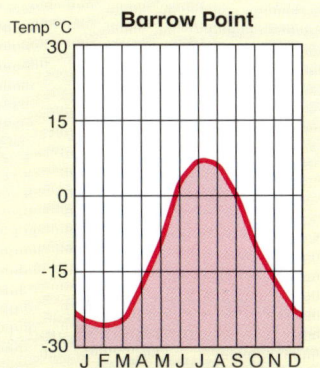

Barrow Point
Buenos Aires
Odessa
Darwin
Temp °C
35
30
15
0
-15
-30
J F M A M J J A S O N D

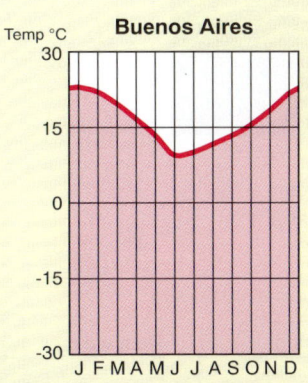

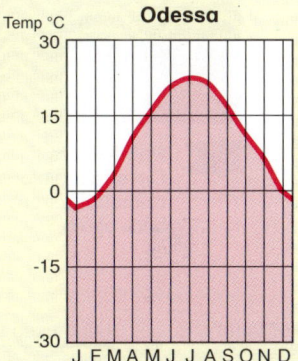

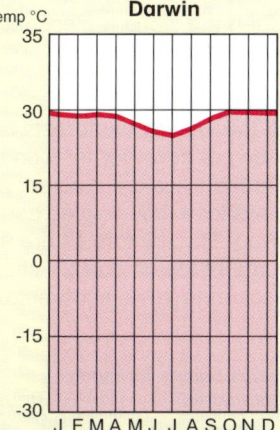

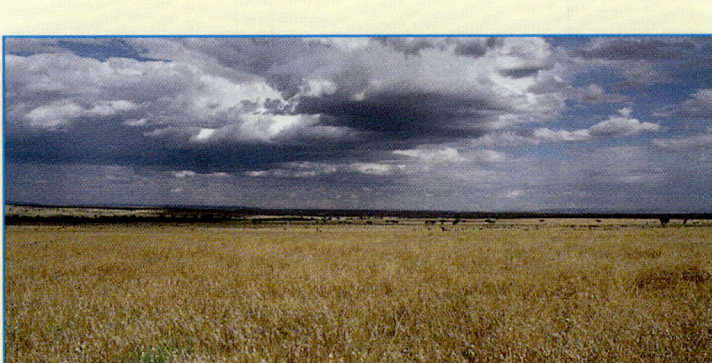

Grassland is typical of moist, warm regions

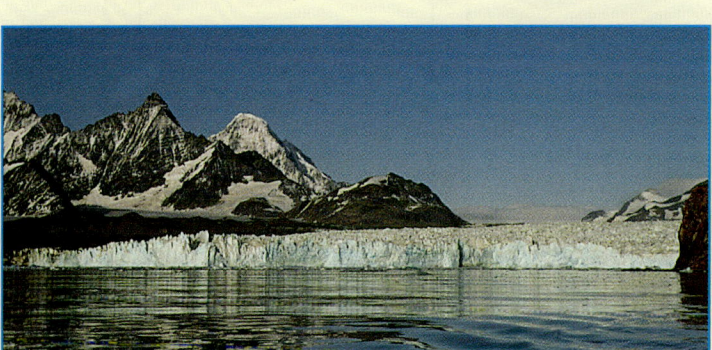

Glaciers are found in very dry, cold regions

64 World Environmental Issues

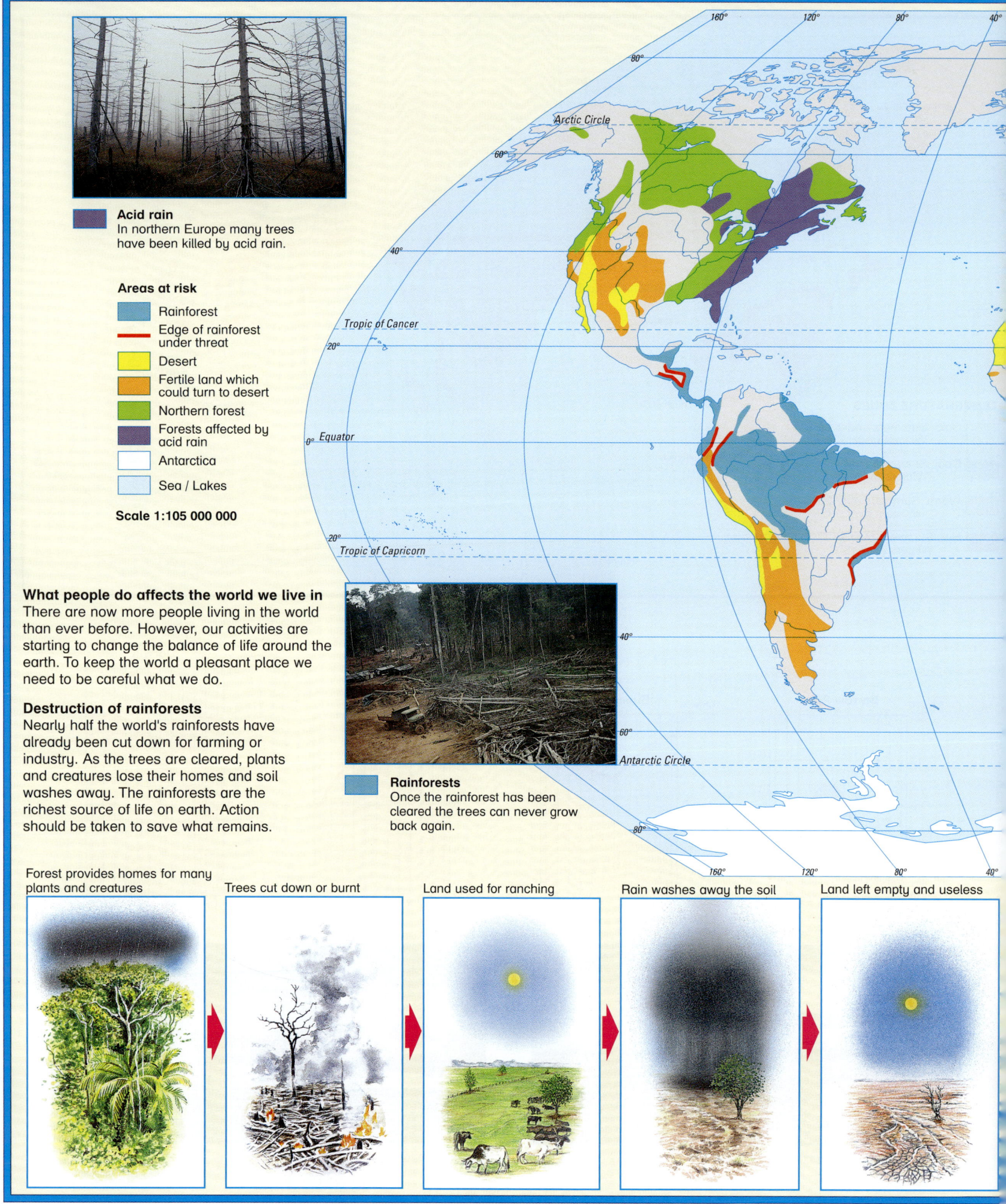

Acid rain
In northern Europe many trees have been killed by acid rain.

Areas at risk
- Rainforest
- Edge of rainforest under threat
- Desert
- Fertile land which could turn to desert
- Northern forest
- Forests affected by acid rain
- Antarctica
- Sea / Lakes

Scale 1:105 000 000

What people do affects the world we live in
There are now more people living in the world than ever before. However, our activities are starting to change the balance of life around the earth. To keep the world a pleasant place we need to be careful what we do.

Destruction of rainforests
Nearly half the world's rainforests have already been cut down for farming or industry. As the trees are cleared, plants and creatures lose their homes and soil washes away. The rainforests are the richest source of life on earth. Action should be taken to save what remains.

Rainforests
Once the rainforest has been cleared the trees can never grow back again.

Forest provides homes for many plants and creatures → Trees cut down or burnt → Land used for ranching → Rain washes away the soil → Land left empty and useless

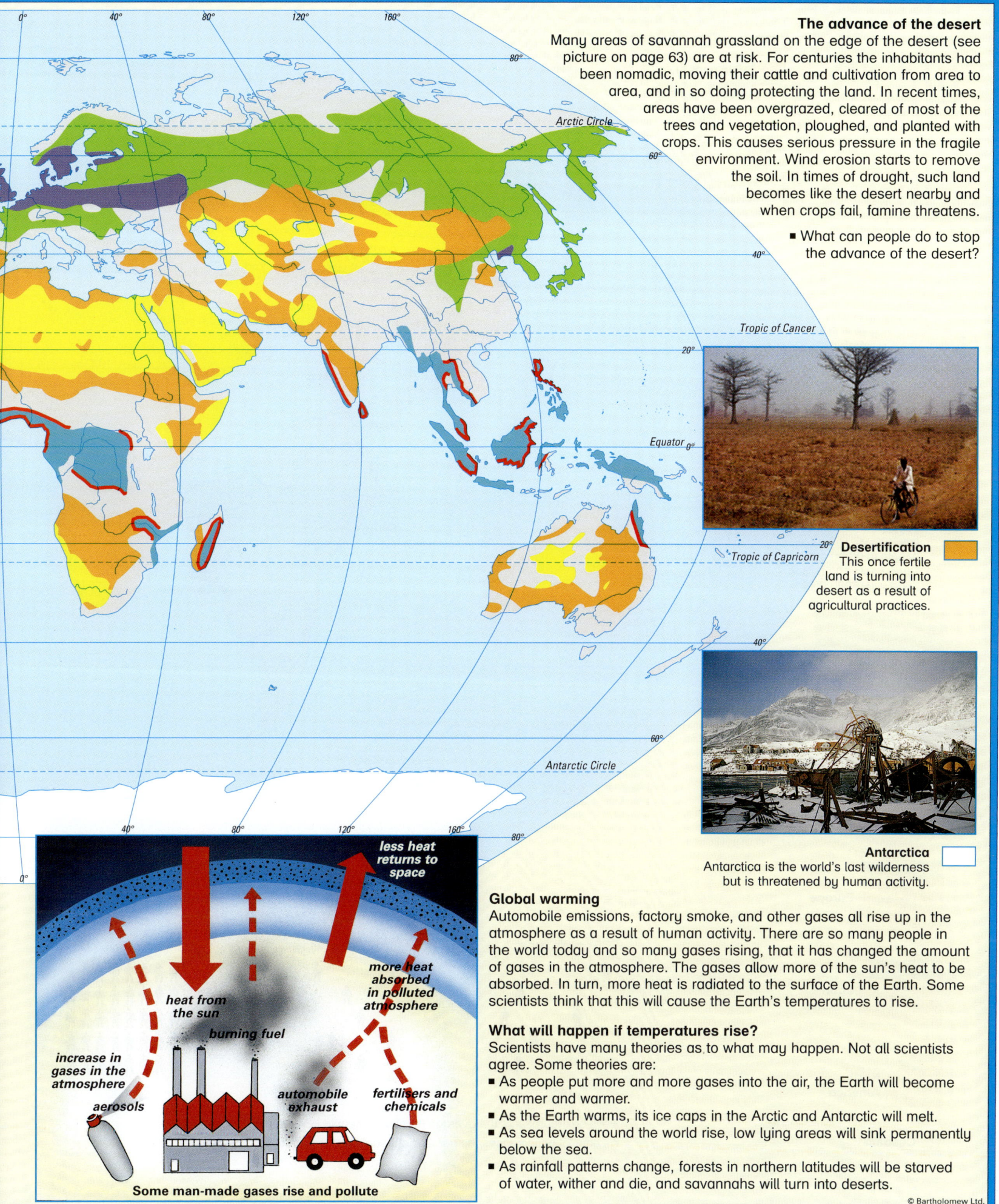

The advance of the desert
Many areas of savannah grassland on the edge of the desert (see picture on page 63) are at risk. For centuries the inhabitants had been nomadic, moving their cattle and cultivation from area to area, and in so doing protecting the land. In recent times, areas have been overgrazed, cleared of most of the trees and vegetation, ploughed, and planted with crops. This causes serious pressure in the fragile environment. Wind erosion starts to remove the soil. In times of drought, such land becomes like the desert nearby and when crops fail, famine threatens.

- What can people do to stop the advance of the desert?

Desertification
This once fertile land is turning into desert as a result of agricultural practices.

Antarctica
Antarctica is the world's last wilderness but is threatened by human activity.

Global warming
Automobile emissions, factory smoke, and other gases all rise up in the atmosphere as a result of human activity. There are so many people in the world today and so many gases rising, that it has changed the amount of gases in the atmosphere. The gases allow more of the sun's heat to be absorbed. In turn, more heat is radiated to the surface of the Earth. Some scientists think that this will cause the Earth's temperatures to rise.

What will happen if temperatures rise?
Scientists have many theories as to what may happen. Not all scientists agree. Some theories are:
- As people put more and more gases into the air, the Earth will become warmer and warmer.
- As the Earth warms, its ice caps in the Arctic and Antarctic will melt.
- As sea levels around the world rise, low lying areas will sink permanently below the sea.
- As rainfall patterns change, forests in northern latitudes will be starved of water, wither and die, and savannahs will turn into deserts.

© Bartholomew Ltd.

World Population

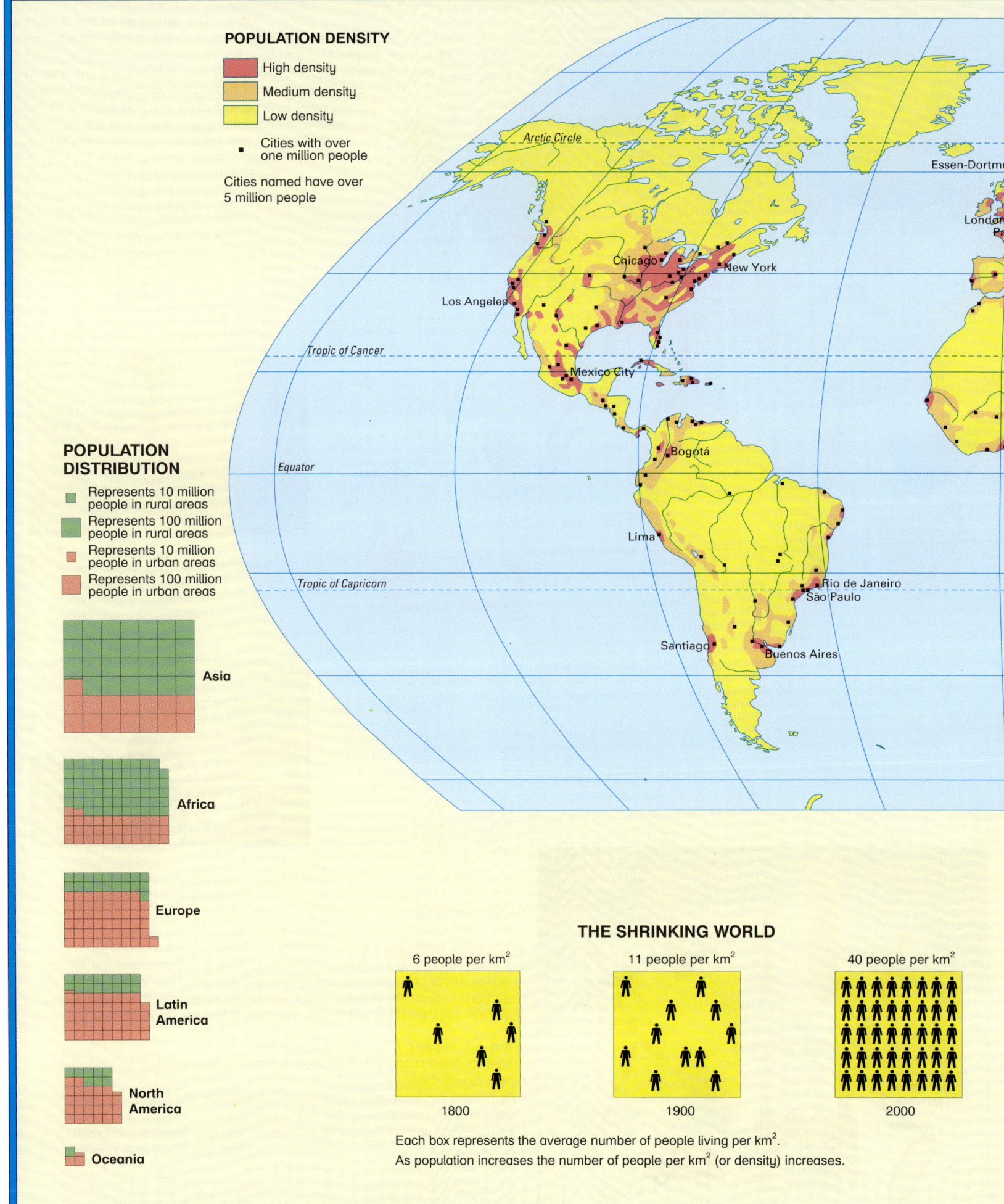

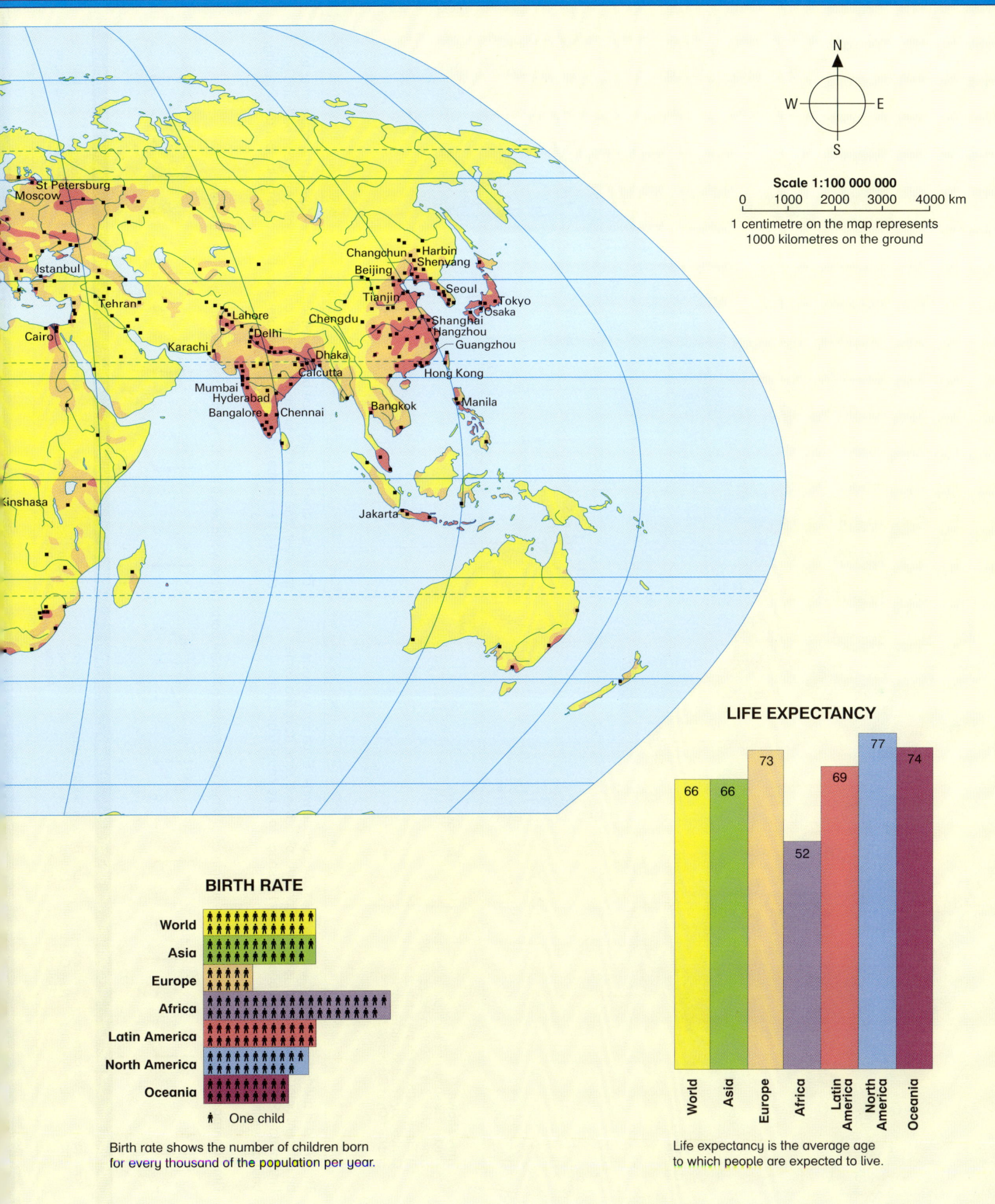

68 Time Zones

There is a one hour difference between each zone – one hour in the day earlier to the west, one hour later to the east. The local time in another city can be found by counting the number of hours earlier or later than the local time in your own country.

Time shown
The time is shown for each of the 24 time zones when it is 06:00h in Belize, 07:00h in Jamaica, 08:00h in the eastern Caribbean, Trinidad and Guyana, and 09:00h in Suriname.

The world is divided into 24 strips, 15 degrees of longitude wide. Each strip (shown by different colours on the map) is a Time Zone. All places in a zone have the same time of day. Some zones have been adjusted in shape to take country and state boundaries into consideration.

Time comparisons The table below gives examples of times observed at different parts of the world when it is 12 noon in the zone at the Prime Meridian.

2:00am	4:00am	6:00am	8:00am	10:00am	12 noon	2:00pm	4:00pm	6:00pm	8:00pm	10:00pm	12 midnight
Hawaiian Is Tahiti	Vancouver Los Angeles	Winnipeg New Orleans Belize City	Puerto Rico La Paz Trinidad	South Georgia	London Rabat Abidjan	Helsinki Cairo Cape Town	Muscat Mauritius	Almaty	Beijing Hong Kong Perth	Port Moresby Sydney	Fiji Auckland

© Collins-Longman Atlases.

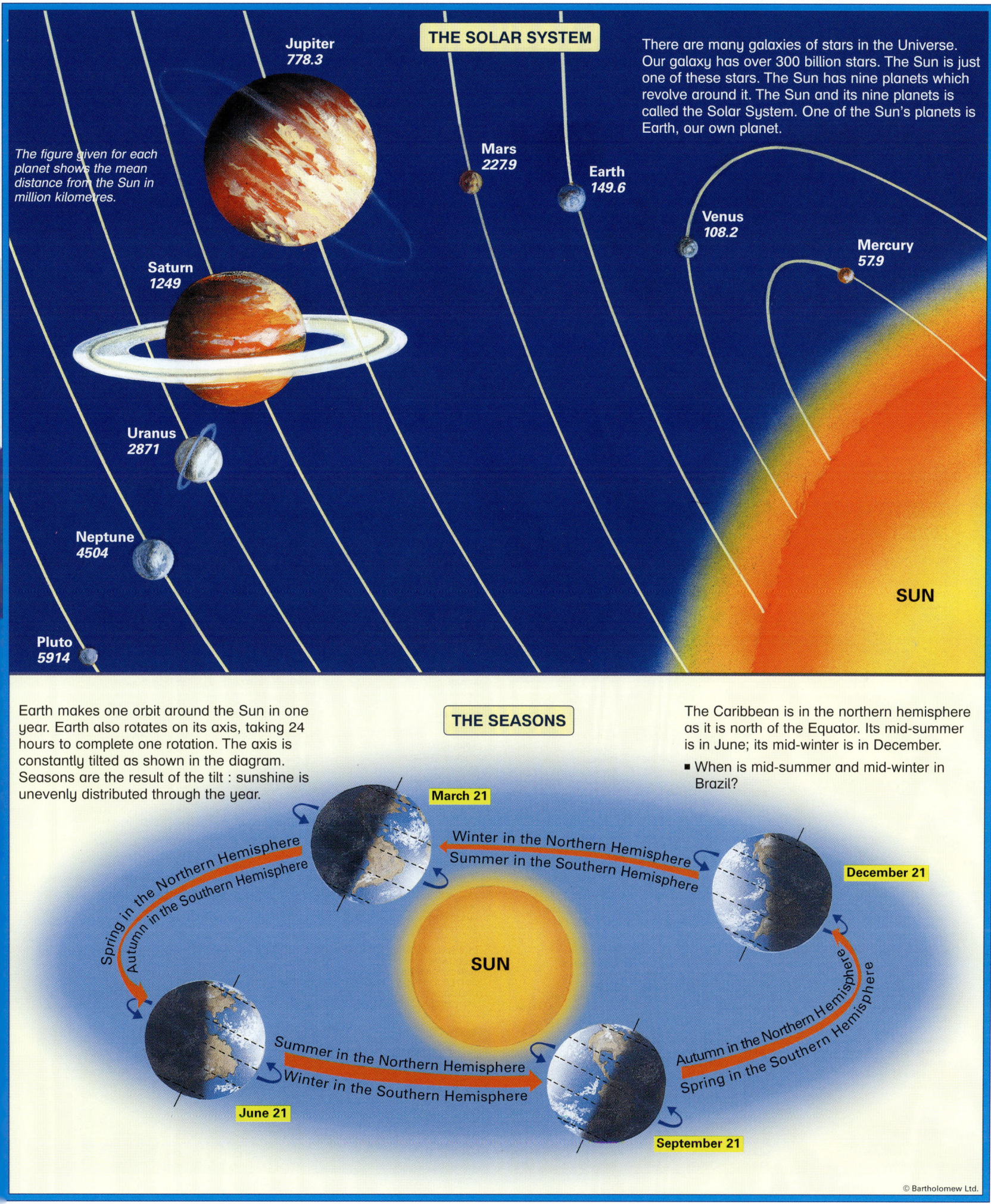

World Facts and Figures

AFRICA

	Population ('000)	Area ('000 sq km)	People per sq km	National capital
ALGERIA	30 081	2 381.7	13	Algiers
ANGOLA	12 092	1 246.7	10	Luanda
BENIN	5 781	112.6	51	PortoNovo
BOTSWANA	1 570	581.4	3	Gaborone
BURKINA	11 305	274.2	41	Ouagadougou
BURUNDI	6 457	27.8	232	Bujumbura
CAMEROON	14 305	475.4	30	Yaoundé
CAPE VERDE	408	4.0	102	Praia
CENTRAL AFRICAN REPUBLIC	3 485	622.4	6	Bangui
CHAD	7 270	1 284.0	6	N'Djamena
COMOROS	658	1.9	346	Moroni
CONGO	2 785	342.0	8	Brazzaville
CÔTE D'IVOIRE	14 292	322.5	44	Yamoussoukro
DEMOCRATIC REPUBLIC OF CONGO	49 139	2 345.4	21	Kinshasa
DJIBOUTI	623	23.2	27	Djibouti
EGYPT	65 978	1 000.3	66	Cairo
EQUATORIAL GUINEA	431	28.1	15	Malabo
ERITREA	3 577	117.4	30	Asmara
ETHIOPIA	59 649	1 133.8	53	Addis Ababa
GABON	1 167	267.7	4	Libreville
GAMBIA	1 229	11.3	109	Banjul
GHANA	19 162	238.5	80	Accra
GUINEA	7 337	245.9	30	Conakry
GUINEA-BISSAU	1 161	36.1	32	Bissau
KENYA	29 008	582.6	50	Nairobi
LESOTHO	2 062	30.3	68	Maseru
LIBERIA	2 666	111.4	24	Monrovia
LIBYA	5 339	1 759.5	3	Tripoli
MADAGASCAR	15 057	587.0	26	Antananarivo
MALAWI	10 346	118.5	87	Lilongwe
MALI	10 694	1 240.1	9	Bamako
MAURITANIA	2 529	1 030.7	2	Nouakchott
MAURITIUS	1 141	2.04	559	Port Louis
MOROCCO	27 377	446.6	61	Rabat
MOZAMBIQUE	18 880	799.4	24	Maputo
NAMIBIA	1 660	824.3	2	Windhoek
NIGER	10 078	1 267.0	8	Niamey
NIGERIA	106 409	923.8	115	Abuja
REPUBLIC OF SOUTH AFRICA	39 357	1 219.1	32	Pretoria/Cape Town
RWANDA	6 604	26.3	251	Kigali
SÃO TOMÉ & PRÍNCIPE	141	0.964	146	São Tomé
SENEGAL	9 003	196.7	46	Dakar
SEYCHELLES	76	0.455	167	Victoria
SIERRA LEONE	4 568	71.7	64	Freetown
SOMALIA	9 237	637.7	14	Mogadishu
SUDAN	28 292	2 505.8	11	Khartoum
SWAZILAND	952	17.4	55	Mbabane
TANZANIA	32 102	945.1	34	Dodoma
TOGO	4 397	56.8	77	Lomé
TUNISIA	9 355	164.2	57	Tunis
UGANDA	20 554	241.0	85	Kampala
WESTERN SAHARA	272	266.0	1	Laâyoune
ZAMBIA	8 781	752.6	12	Lusaka
ZIMBABWE	11 377	390.8	29	Harare

EUROPE

	Population ('000)	Area ('000 sq km)	People per sq km	National capital
ALBANIA	3 119	28.7	109	Tiranë
ANDORRA	72	0.465	155	Andorra la Vella
AUSTRIA	8 140	83.9	97	Vienna
BELARUS	10 315	207.6	50	Minsk
BELGIUM	10 141	30.5	332	Brussels
BOSNIA-HERZEGOVINA	3 675	51.1	72	Sarajevo
BULGARIA	8 336	111.0	75	Sofia
CROATIA	4 481	56.5	79	Zagreb
CZECH REPUBLIC	10 282	78.9	130	Prague
DENMARK	5 270	43.1	122	Copenhagen
ESTONIA	1 429	45.2	32	Tallinn
FINLAND	5 154	338.1	15	Helsinki
FRANCE	58 683	544.0	108	Paris
GERMANY	82 133	357.0	230	Berlin
GREECE	10 600	132.0	80	Athens
HUNGARY	10 116	93.0	109	Budapest
ICELAND	276	102.8	3	Reykjavik
ITALY	57 369	301.2	190	Rome
LATVIA	2 424	63.7	38	Riga
LIECHTENSTEIN	32	0.160	200	Vaduz
LITHUANIA	3 694	65.2	57	Vilnius
LUXEMBOURG	422	2.6	162	Luxembourg
MACEDONIA	1 999	25.7	78	Skopje
MALTA	384	0.316	1 215	Valletta
MOLDOVA	4 378	33.7	130	Chişinău
NETHERLANDS	15 678	41.5	378	Amsterdam/The Hague
NORWAY	4 419	323.9	14	Oslo
POLAND	38 718	312.7	124	Warsaw
PORTUGAL	9 869	88.9	111	Lisbon
REPUBLIC OF IRELAND	3 681	70.3	52	Dublin
ROMANIA	22 474	237.5	95	Bucharest
RUSSIAN FEDERATION	147 434	17 075.4	9	Moscow
SLOVAKIA	5 377	49.0	110	Bratislava
SLOVENIA	1 993	20.3	98	Ljubljana
SPAIN	39 628	504.8	79	Madrid
SWEDEN	8 875	450.0	20	Stockholm
SWITZERLAND	7 299	41.3	177	Bern
UKRAINE	50 861	603.7	84	Kiev
UNITED KINGDOM	58 649	244.1	240	London
YUGOSLAVIA	10 635	102.2	104	Belgrade

ASIA

	Population ('000)	Area ('000 sq km)	People per sq km	National capital
AFGHANISTAN	21 354	652.2	33	Kabul
ARMENIA	3 536	29.8	119	Yerevan
AZERBAIJAN	7 669	86.6	89	Baku
BAHRAIN	595	0.691	861	Manama
BANGLADESH	124 774	144.0	866	Dhaka
BHUTAN	2 004	46.6	43	Thimbu
BRUNEI	315	5.8	54	Bandar Seri Begawan
CAMBODIA	10 716	181.0	59	Phnom Penh
CHINA	1 262 817	9 584.5	132	Beijing
CYPRUS	771	9.2	84	Nicosia
GEORGIA	5 059	69.7	73	Tbilisi
INDIA	982 223	3 065.0	320	New Delhi
INDONESIA	206 338	1 919.4	108	Jakarta
IRAN	65 758	1 648.0	40	Teheran
IRAQ	21 800	438.3	50	Baghdad
ISRAEL	5 984	20.8	288	Jerusalem
JAPAN	126 281	377.7	334	Tokyo
JORDAN	6 304	89.2	71	Amman
KAZAKHSTAN	16 319	2 717.3	6	Astana
KUWAIT	1 811	17.8	102	Kuwait
KYRGYZSTAN	4 643	198.5	23	Bishkek
LAOS	5 163	236.8	22	Vientiane
LEBANON	3 191	10.5	304	Beirut
MALAYSIA	21 410	333.0	64	Kuala Lumpur
MONGOLIA	2 579	1 565.0	2	Ulan-Bator
MYANMAR	44 497	676.6	66	Yangon
NEPAL	22 847	147.2	155	Kathmandu
NORTH KOREA	23 348	120.5	194	Pyongyang
OMAN	2 382	309.5	8	Muscat
PAKISTAN	148 166	803.9	184	Islamabad
PHILIPPINES	72 944	300.0	243	Manila
QATAR	579	11.4	51	Doha
SAUDI ARABIA	20 181	2200	9	Riyadh
SINGAPORE	3 476	0.639	5 440	Singapore
SOUTH KOREA	46 109	99.3	464	Seoul
SRI LANKA	18 455	65.6	281	Colombo/Kotte
SYRIA	15 333	185.2	83	Damascus
TAIWAN	21 908	36.2	605	Taibei
TAJIKISTAN	6 015	143.1	42	Dushanbe
THAILAND	60 300	513.1	118	Bangkok
TURKEY	64 479	779.5	83	Ankara
TURKMENISTAN	4 309	488.1	9	Ashgabat
UNITED ARAB EMIRATES	2 377	83.6	28	Abu Dhabi
UZBEKISTAN	23 574	447.4	53	Tashkent
VIETNAM	77 562	329.6	235	Hanoi
YEMEN	16 887	528.0	32	San'a

NORTH AMERICA & SOUTH AMERICA

	Population ('000)	Area ('000 sq km)	People per sq km	National capital
ANTIGUA AND BARBUDA	68	0.442	154	St John's
ARGENTINA	36 123	2 766.9	13	Buenos Aires
BAHAMAS	309	13.9	22	Nassau
BARBADOS	260	0.430	605	Bridgetown
BELIZE	250	23.0	11	Belmopan
BERMUDA	63	0.054	1 167	Hamilton
BOLIVIA	7 957	1 098.6	7	La Paz/Sucre
BRAZIL	165 851	8 547.4	19	Brasilia
CANADA	30 563	9 970.6	3	Ottawa
CHILE	14 824	756.9	20	Santiago
COLOMBIA	40 803	1 141.7	36	Bogotá
COSTA RICA	3 841	51.1	75	San José
CUBA	11 260	110.9	102	Havana
DOMINICA	72	0.750	96	Roseau
DOMINICAN REPUBLIC	8 700	48.4	180	Santo Domingo
ECUADOR	12 175	272.0	45	Quito
EL SALVADOR	6 032	21.0	287	San Salvador
FRENCH GUIANA	167	90.0	2	Cayenne
GRENADA	95	0.345	275	St George's
GUATEMALA	10 801	108.9	99	Guatemala City
GUYANA	725	215.0	3	Georgetown
HAITI	8 000	27.8	292	Port-au-Prince
HONDURAS	6 147	112.1	55	Tegucigalpa
JAMAICA	2 750	11.0	250	Kingston
MEXICO	95 831	1 972.5	49	Mexico City
NICARAGUA	4 807	130.0	37	Managua
PANAMA	2 767	77.1	36	Panamá City
PARAGUAY	5 222	406.8	13	Asunción
PERU	24 797	1 285.2	19	Lima
PUERTO RICO	3 960	9.0	435	San Juan
ST KITTS AND NEVIS	41	0.262	157	Basseterre
ST LUCIA	150	0.616	244	Castries
ST VINCENT AND THE GRENADINES	115	0.389	296	Kingstown
SURINAME	414	163.8	3	Paramaribo
TRINIDAD AND TOBAGO	1 330	5.1	261	Port of Spain
UNITED STATES OF AMERICA	274 028	9 809.4	28	Washington
URUGUAY	3 289	176.2	19	Montevideo
VENEZUELA	23 242	912.0	25	Caracas

OCEANIA

	Population ('000)	Area ('000 sq km)	People per sq km	National capital
AUSTRALIA	18 520	7 682.3	2	Canberra
FIJI	796	18.3	43	Suva
KIRIBATI	81	0.717	113	Bairiki
NAURU	11	0.021	524	Yaren
NEW ZEALAND	3 796	270.5	14	Wellington
PAPUA NEW GUINEA	4 600	462.8	10	Port Moresby
SAMOA	174	2.8	62	Apia
SOLOMON ISLANDS	417	28.4	15	Honiara
TONGA	98	0.748	131	Nuku'alofa
TUVALU	11	0.025	440	Vaiaku
VANUATU	182	12.2	15	Port Vila

© Bartholomew Ltd.

Index 71

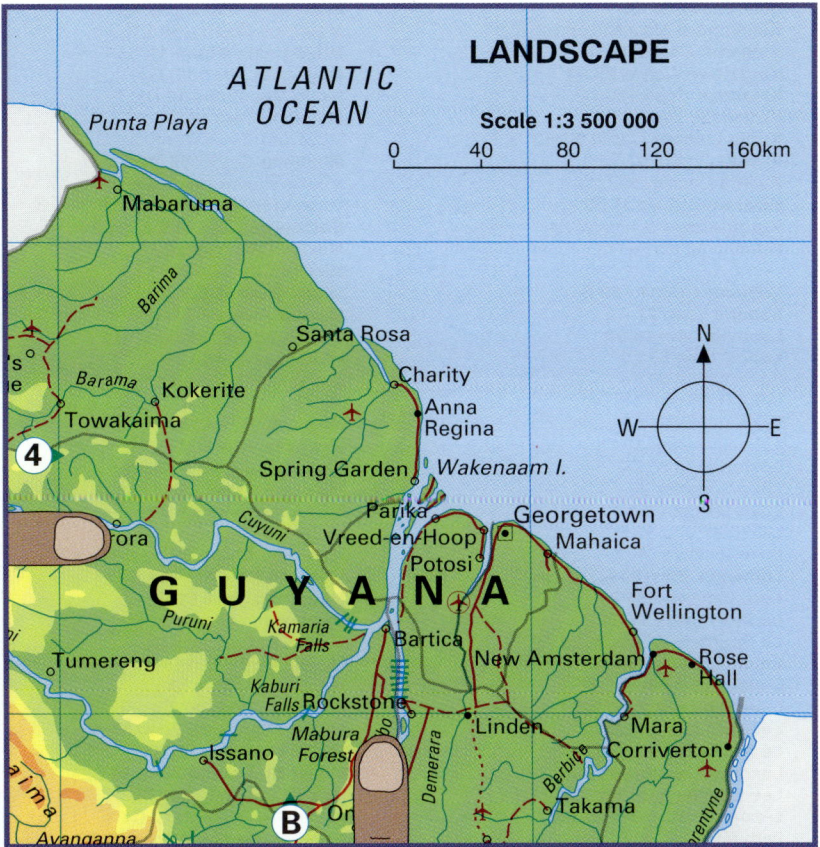

Colour coding of places
All the places in this index are colour-coded. Places printed in black are physical features of the landscape such as islands, reefs, mountains, highlands, hills, peaks, ridges, peninsulas, reefs, deserts, and natural regions. Places printed in blue are water features such as oceans, seas, rivers, lakes, passages between islands, gulfs and bays. Red shows countries and self-governing overseas territories. Green shows cities and towns, including the capitals of countries and territories.

Using the index of places
You can use this **index** to help you find places in this atlas. The index has many - but not all - of the places named on the Caribbean maps, and the most important places on the maps of the rest of the world. For each place named in the index you are told whether it is a country, capital, town, island, river, or mountain. Then you are told the page with the best map in the atlas to find the place. The index also gives **grid squares** which help you to know where on the map to find the place. There are numbers at the sides and letters at the bottom of the pages showing landscape and political maps for identifying the grid squares.

Example: **Georgetown** *Capital* **37** B4
Explanation: Georgetown is a capital city. The best map to find it is on page 37, in grid square B4.

This is how you find where Georgetown is on the map using the grid square. Practise these steps.

- Put the index finger of your right hand beside **B** at the bottom of the map.
- Put the index finger of your left hand beside **4** at the left side of the map.
- Move your right hand index finger UP THE MAP, and your left hand index finger TO THE RIGHT.
- Your fingers will meet in the grid square with Georgetown.

Abidjan *Town* 59 B3
Abuja *Capital* 59 C3
Accra *Capital* 59 B3
Acklins Island 10 F5
Aconcagua *Mountain* 52 B2
Addis Ababa *Capital* 59 D3
Adelaide *Town* 61 C2
Afghanistan *Country* 57 D3
Aishalton *Town* 37 B2
Albania *Country* 55 E2
Alexandria *Town* 59 D4
Algeria *Country* 59 C4
Algiers *Capital* 59 C4
Alice Springs *Town* 61 C3
All Saints *Town* 24 D3
Almaty *Town* 57 E4
Alps *Mountains* 54 D2
Altai Mountains 56 F4
Amazon *River* 52 C4
Ambergis Cay *Island* 12 D6
Amman *Capital* 57 C3
Amsterdam *Capital* 55 D3
Amuku Mountains 34 B1
Andes *Mountains* 52 B3
Andorra *Country* 55 D2
Andros Island 10 D6
Anegada *Island* 21 D3
Angola *Country* 59 C2
Anguilla *Territory* 21 Z5
Ankara *Capital* 57 C3
Anna Regina *Town* 37 B4
Annotto Bay *Town* 15 D2
Anse Du Mé *Town* 26 A3
Anse la Raye *Town* 27 A2
Antananarivo *Capital* 59 E2
Antigua and Barbuda *Country* 24
Appalachian Mountains 50 F2
Arabia *Peninsula* 56 C3
Arabian Sea 56 D2
Arctic Ocean 50 B4
Argentina *Country* 53 B3
Arima *Town* 32 C3
Armenia *Country* 57 C4
Arouca *Town* 32 C3
Aruba *Island* 19
Ashgabat *Capital* 57 D3
Asmara *Capital* 59 D3
Astana *Capital* 57 E4
Asunción *Capital* 53 C3
Athens *Capital* 55 F1
Atlantic Ocean 46 G5

Atlas Mountains 58 B4
Auckland *Town* 61 G2
Aurora *Town* 37 B4
Australia *Country* 61 C3
Austria *Country* 55 E2
Azerbaijan *Country* 57 C4

Baffin Island 50 G4
Baghdad *Capital* 57 C3
Bahamas, The *Country* 10 F6
Bahrain *Country* 57 D3
Baku *Town* 57 C4
Balaclava *Town* 14 B2
Bamako *Capital* 59 B3
Bangkok *Capital* 57 F2
Bangladesh *Country* 57 E3
Bangui *Capital* 59 C3
Banjul *Capital* 59 B3
Barama *River* 37 B4
Barbados *Country* 30
Barcelona *Town* 55 D2
Barima *River* 37 B5
Barranquilla *Town* 53 B4
Barrouallie *Town* 28 A2
Bartica *Town* 37 B4
Basseterre *Capital* 22 B2
Basse-Terre *Capital* 25 A1
Basse-Terre *Island* 25 A2
Bath *Town* 15 E1
Bayamo *Town* 10 E4
Beijing *Capital* 57 G3
Belair *Town* 30 B2
Belarus *Country* 55 F3
Belfast *Town* 55 C3
Belgium *Country* 55 D3
Belgrade *Capital* 55 F2
Belize *Country* 12
Belize *River* 12 C5
Belize City *Town* 12 C4
Belmopan *Capital* 12 B4
Belo Horizonte *Town* 53 C3
Benin *Country* 59 C3
Bequia *Island* 28 Y4
Berbice *River* 37 C4
Berekua *Town* 26 B1
Berlin *Capital* 55 E3
Bermuda *Territory* 50 G2
Bern *Capital* 55 D2
Bhutan *Country* 57 F3
Big Creek *Town* 12 C3
Bishkek *Capital* 57 E4

Bissau *Capital* 59 B3
Black River *Town* 14 B2
Black Sea 54 G2
Blowing Point *Town* 21 Y5
Blue Mountains 15 D2
Blue Mountains Peak 15 D2
Bogota *Capital* 8 E1
Bog Walk *Town* 15 C2
Bolans *Town* 24 C3
Bolivia *Country* 53 B4
Bonaire *Island* 19
Bonn *Town* 55 D3
Borneo *Island* 56 G1
Bosnia-Herzegovina *Country* 55 E2
Botswana *Country* 59 D1
Brasília *Capital* 53 C4
Bratislava *Capital* 55 E2
Brazil *Country* 53 C4
Brazilian Highlands 52 C3
Brazzaville *Capital* 59 C2
Bridgetown *Capital* 30 A2
Brisbane *Town* 61 E3
British Virgin Islands *Territory* 21
Browns Town 14 C2
Brunei *Country* 57 G2
Brussels *Capital* 55 D3
Buccoo *Town* 36 B2
Bucharest *Capital* 55 F2
Budapest *Capital* 55 E2
Buena Vista *Town* 12 B6
Buenos Aires *Capital* 53 C3
Buff Bay *Town* 15 D2
Bujumbura *Capital* 59 D2
Bulgaria *Country* 55 F2
Burkina *Country* 59 B3
Burundi *Country* 59 D2

Caicos Islands 11 H4
Caicos Passage 11 G5
Cairo *Capital* 59 D4
Calcutta *Town* 57 E3
Cali *Town* 53 B4
Camagüey *Town* 10 E4
Cambodia *Country* 57 F2
Cambridge *Town* 14 B2
Cameroon *Country* 59 C3
Canada *Country* 51 E3
Canaries *Town* 27 A2
Canberra *Capital* 61 D2
Canefield *Town* 26 A1
Canouan *Island* 20 B1

Capesterre-Belle-Eau *Town* 25 A2
Cape Town *Capital* 59 C1
Cape Verde *Country* 59 A3
Caracas *Capital* 9 F3
Caribbean Sea 8 D4
Carlisle Bay 30 A2
Caroni *River* 32 C3
Carpathian Mountains 54 F2
Carriacou *Island* 29 C5
Cartagena *Town* 8 D3
Casablanca *Town* 59 B4
Caspian Sea 56 D3
Castara *Town* 36 C3
Castries *Capital* 27 A3
Catherines Peak 15 D2
Cat Island 10 F6
Cayenne *Capital* 9 I1
Cayman Brac *Island* 13 Y1
Cayman Islands *Territory* 13
Cayon *Town* 22 B3
Central African Republic *Country* 59 C3
Central Range *Mountains* 32 C2
Chad *Country* 59 C3
Challengers *Town* 22 B2
Chances Peak *Mountain* 23 A1
Chang Jiang *River* 56 G3
Chapelton *Town* 15 C2
Charity *Town* 37 B4
Charlestown *Town* 22 C1
Charlotte Amalie *Capital* 21 B2
Chateaubelair *Town* 28 A2
Chicago *Town* 51 F3
Chile *Country* 53 B3
China *Country* 57 F3
Chisinau *Capital* 55 F2
Choiseul *Town* 27 A1
Christchurch *Town* 61 G1
Christiana *Town* 14 C2
Cienfuegos *Town* 10 C5
Cocos Bay 32 D2
Codrington *Town* 24 B1
Colombia *Country* 53 B5
Colombo *Town* 57 E2
Colorado *River* 50 E2
Comoros *Country* 59 E2
Conakry *Capital* 59 B3
Congo *River* 58 C2
Congo *Country* 59 C2
Constitution *River* 30 A2
Copenhagen *Capital* 55 E3

Index

Corentyne *River* 37 C3
Corozal *Town* 12 C6
Corriverton *Town* 37 C3
Costa Rica *Country* 8 C3
Cote d'Ivoire *Country* 59 B3
Cotton Ground *Town* 22 C2
Couva *Town* 32 C2
Crete *Island* 55 F1
Croatia *Country* 55 E2
Crooked Island 10 F5
Cuba *Country* 10 D4
Curaçao *Island* 19
Curitiba *Town* 53 C2
Cuyuni *River* 37 B4
Cyprus *Country* 57 C3
Czech Republic *Country* 55 E2

Dakar *Capital* 59 B3
Damascus *Capital* 57 C3
Dangriga *Town* 12 C3
Danube *River* 54 F2
Dar es Salaam *Town* 59 D2
Darling *River* 60 D2
Darwin *Town* 61 C4
Delhi *Town* 57 E3
Demerara *River* 37 B4
Democratic Republic of Congo *Country* 59 D2
Denmark *Country* 55 D3
Dennery *Town* 27 B2
Dhaka *Capital* 57 E3
Diego Martin *Town* 32 B3
Djibouti *Capital* 59 E3
Djibouti *Country* 59 E3
Dodoma *Capital* 59 D2
Dominica *Country* 26
Dominican Republic *Country* 11 H3
Dry Harbour Mountains 14 C2
Dublin *Capital* 55 C3
Dulcina *Town* 24 B1
Durban *Town* 59 D1
Dushanbe *Capital* 57 D3

East Caicos *Island* 11 H4
Ecuador *Country* 53 B4
Edinburgh *Town* 55 C3
Egypt *Country* 59 D4
Eleuthera Island 10 E6
El Salvador *Country* 8 B3
English Harbour Town 24 D3
Equatorial Guinea *Country* 59 C3
Eritrea *Country* 59 D3
Essequibo *River* 37 B4
Estonia *Country* 55 F3
Ethiopia *Country* 59 D3
Ethiopian Highlands 58 D3
Ewarton *Town* 15 C2

Falkland Islands *Territory* 52 C1
Falmouth *Town* 14 B2
Fiji *Country* 61 G4
Finland *Country* 55 F4
Five Islands Village *Town* 24 C3
Fort-de-France *Capital* 25 C5
Fort Wellington *Town* 37 C4
France *Country* 55 D2
Frankfield *Town* 14 C2
Freetown *Capital* 59 B3
French Guiana *Country* 9 I1
Frigate Bay *Town* 22 B2

Gabon *Country* 59 C2
Gaborone *Capital* 59 D1
Gambia *Country* 59 B3
Ganges *River* 56 E3
Garrison *Town* 30 A1
Gayle *Town* 15 C2
George Town *Capital* 13 A1
Georgetown *Capital* 37 B4
Georgetown *Town* 28 B2
Georgeville *Town* 12 B4
Georgia *Country* 57 C4
Germany *Country* 55 E3
Ghana *Country* 59 B3
Gibraltar *Territory* 55 C1
Gobi *Desert* 56 F4
Golden Grove *Town* 15 E1
Gosier *Town* 25 B2
Gouyave *Town* 29 A2
Grand Bahama Island 10 D7
Grand Cayman *Island* 13 C3
Grande-Terre *Island* 25 B2

Grand Turk *Island* 11 H4
Grange Hill *Town* 14 A2
Great Abaco Island 10 E7
Great Barrier Reef 60 D4
Great Dividing Range *Mountains* 60 D3
Greater Antilles *Islands* 10
Great Exuma Island 10 F5
Great Inagua Island 11 G4
Great Rift Valley 58 D2
Great Victoria Desert 60 B3
Greece *Country* 55 F1
Greenland *Country* 51 H4
Grenada *Country* 29 A2
Grenadine Islands 28
Grenville *Town* 29 B2
Gros Islet *Town* 27 B3
Guadalajara *Town* 51 E2
Guadeloupe *Island* 25
Guantanamo *Town* 10 F4
Guatemala *Country* 8 A4
Guatemala City *Capital* 8 A3
Guatuaro *River* 32 D1
Guinea *Country* 59 B3
Guinea Bissau *Country* 59 B3
Gulf of Guinea 58 B3
Gulf of Mexico 50 F2
Gulf of Paria 32 B2
Gustavia *Town* 19 Z7
Guyana *Country* 37

Haiti *Country* 11 G3
Half Way Tree *Town* 15 D2
Hamburg *Town* 55 D3
Hanoi *Capital* 57 F3
Harare *Capital* 59 D2
Hastings *Town* 30 A1
Hattieville *Town* 12 C4
Havana *Capital* 10 B5
Hayes *Town* 15 C1
Hellshire Hills 15 D1
Helsinki *Capital* 55 F4
Highgate *Town* 15 D2
Himalaya *Mountains* 56 E3
Hispaniola *Island* 11 H3
Hobart *Town* 61 D1
Hokkaido *Island* 56 H4
Holetown *Town* 30 A3
Holguin *Town* 10 E4
Honduras *Country* 8 B3
Hong Kong *Town* 57 G3
Honiara *Capital* 61 E5
Honshu *Island* 56 H3
Houston *Town* 51 F2
Huang He *River* 56 G3
Hudson Bay 50 F3
Hungary *Country* 55 E2
Hyderabad *Town* 57 E2

Ibadan *Town* 59 C3
Iceland *Country* 55 B4
India *Country* 57 E3
Indian Ocean 56 E2
Indonesia *Country* 57 F1
Indus *River* 56 D3
Iran *Country* 57 D3
Iraq *Country* 57 C3
Ireland *Country* 55 C3
Isherton *Town* 37 B2
Islamabad *Capital* 57 E3
Israel *Country* 57 C3
Istanbul *Town* 55 F2
Italy *Country* 55 E2
Ituni *Town* 37 B3

Jakarta *Capital* 57 F1
Jamaica *Country* 14-15
Japan *Country* 57 H3
Java *Island* 56 F1
Johannesburg *Town* 59 D1
John Crow Mountains 15 E2
Jordan *Country* 57 C3

Kabul *Capital* 57 D3
Kalahari Desert 58 D1
Kamarang *Town* 37 A3
Kampala *Capital* 59 D3
Karachi *Town* 57 D3
Kathmandu *Capital* 57 E3
Kazakhstan *Country* 57 D4
Kellits *Town* 15 C2
Kenya *Country* 59 D3
Khartoum *Capital* 59 D3

Kiev *Capital* 55 G3
Kilimanjaro *Mountain* 58 D2
Kingston *Capital* 15 D1
Kingstown *Capital* 28 A1
Kinshasa *Capital* 59 C2
Kralendijk *Town* 19 D1
Kuala Lumpur *Capital* 57 F2
Kuwait *Capital* 57 C3
Kuwait *Country* 57 C3
Kwakwani *Town* 37 B3
Kyrgyzstan *Country* 57 E4
Kyushu *Island* 56 H3

Laâyoune *Capital* 59 B4
Laborie *Town* 27 A1
Lacovia *Town* 14 B2
Lagos *Town* 59 C3
Lake Baikal 56 F4
Lake Balkhash 56 E4
Lake Huron 50 F3
Lake Michigan 50 F3
Lake Nyasa 58 D2
Lake Superior 50 F3
Lake Tanganyika 58 D2
Lake Titicaca 52 B3
Lake Victoria 58 D2
Lamentin *Town* 25 A2
Laos *Country* 57 F2
La Paz *Capital* 53 B4
La Soufrière *Mountain* 25 A2
Latvia *Country* 55 F3
Layou *Town* 28 A2
Lebanon *Country* 57 C3
Leeward Islands 20 B3
Le Moule *Town* 25 B2
Lesotho *Country* 59 D1
Les Saintes *Islands* 25 A1
Lesser Antilles *Islands* 9 G4
Lethem *Town* 37 B2
Liberia *Country* 59 B3
Liberta *Town* 24 D3
Libreville *Capital* 59 C3
Libya *Country* 59 C4
Lilongwe *Capital* 59 D2
Lima *Capital* 53 B4
Linden *Town* 37 B4
Linstead *Town* 15 C2
Lisbon *Capital* 55 C1
Lithuania *Country* 55 F3
Little Cayman *Island* 13 W2
Ljubljana *Capital* 55 E2
Lomé *Capital* 59 C3
London *Capital* 55 D3
Long Island 10 F5
Los Angeles *Town* 51 E2
Loubière *Town* 26 A1
Luanda *Capital* 59 C2
Lucea *Town* 14 A2
Lusaka *Capital* 59 D2
Luxembourg *Country* 55 D2
Luzon *Island* 56 G2

Macedonia *Country* 55 F2
Madagascar *Country* 59 E1
Madrid *Capital* 55 C2
Mahaica *Town* 37 C4
Main Ridge *Mountains* 36 D3
Malabo *Capital* 59 C3
Malawi *Country* 59 D2
Malaysia *Country* 57 F2
Maldives *Country* 57 E2
Mali *Country* 59 B3
Malta *Country* 44 E1
Managua *Capital* 8 B3
Mandeville *Town* 14 B2
Manila *Capital* 57 G2
Mapp Hill *Town* 30 B2
Maputo *Capital* 59 D1
Mara *Town* 37 C3
Maracaibo *Town* 53 B5
Margarita Island 9 G3
Marie Galante *Island* 25 B1
Marigot *Capital* 21 Y4
Marigot *Town* 26 B3
Marquis *Town* 27 B3
Marseille *Town* 55 D2
Martinique *Island* 25
Maseru *Capital* 59 D1
Maskall *Town* 12 C5
Matanzas *Town* 10 C5
Matthew's Ridge *Town* 37 A4
Matura Bay 32 D3

Mauritania *Country* 59 B4
Mauritius *Country* 59 E1
Mayaguana Island 11 G5
Mayagüez *Town* 11 J3
Maya Mountains 12 B3
May Pen *Town* 15 C1
Mazaruni *River* 37 B4
Mbabane *Capital* 59 D1
Mediterranean Sea 54 E1
Mekong *River* 56 F2
Melbourne *Town* 61 D2
Mexico *Country* 51 E2
Mexico City *Capital* 51 F1
Miami *Town* 51 F2
Micoud *Town* 27 B1
Middle Caicos *Island* 11 H4
Middlesex *Town* 12 B4
Minneapolis *Town* 51 F3
Minsk *Capital* 55 F3
Mississippi *River* 50 F2
Missouri *River* 50 F3
Mogadishu *Capital* 59 E3
Moldova *Country* 55 F2
Mombasa *Town* 59 D2
Mongolia *Country* 57 F4
Monrovia *Capital* 59 B3
Montego Bay *Town* 14 B2
Monterrey *Town* 51 E2
Montevideo *Capital* 53 C3
Montserrat *Territory* 23
Morant Bay *Town* 15 E1
Morocco *Country* 59 B4
Moscow *Capital* 57 C4
Mount Friendship *Town* 30 A2
Mount McKinley 50 C4
Mount St. George *Town* 36 C2
Mozambique *Country* 59 D2
Mullins River *Town* 12 C4
Mumbai (Bombay) *Town* 57 E2
Munich *Town* 55 E2
Murray *River* 60 D2
Muscat *Capital* 57 D3
Mustique *Island* 28 Y3
Myanmar *Country* 57 F3

Nairobi *Capital* 59 D2
Namibia *Country* 59 C1
Nassau *Capital* 10 E6
N'Djamena *Capital* 59 C3
Negril *Town* 14 A2
Nepal *Country* 57 E3
Netherlands *Country* 55 D3
Netherlands Antilles *Islands* 19
Nevis *Island* 22 C1
New Amsterdam *Town* 37 C4
New Caledonia *Island* 60 F3
New Delhi *Capital* 57 E3
Newfoundland *Island* 50 H3
New Guinea *Island* 60 D5
New Orleans *Town* 51 F2
New Providence Island 10 E6
Newton Ground *Town* 22 A3
New York *Town* 51 G3
New Zealand *Country* 61 G1
Niamey *Capital* 59 C3
Nicaragua *Country* 8 B3
Niger *Country* 59 C3
Niger *River* 58 C3
Nigeria *Country* 59 C3
Nile *River* 58 D4
North Caicos *Island* 11 H4
Northern Range *Mountains* 32 C3
North Korea *Country* 57 G3
North Sea 54 D3
Norway *Country* 55 E4
Nouakchott *Capital* 59 B3
Novosibirsk *Town* 57 E4
Nuuk (Godthåb) *Capital* 51 H4

Ob *River* 56 D5
Ocho Rios *Town* 15 C2
Odessa *Town* 55 G2
Oistins *Town* 30 B1
Old Harbour *Town* 15 C1
Old Road Town 22 B2
Oman *Country* 57 D2
Orange *River* 58 C1
Orange Walk *Town* 12 B6
Oranjestad *Capital* 19 F4
Orinoco *River* 9 G2
Osaka *Town* 57 H3
Oslo *Capital* 55 E3